W9-ADJ-443

Dangerous Drugs

"*Dangerous Drugs* provides a useful, up-to-date reference for parents and professionals. It is a valuable antidote to the facile and frighteningly misleading pro-drug propaganda all too available on the Internet. The short summary of this valuable book: Drugs really *are* dangerous. After thirty years working in drug abuse prevention, I offer a heartfelt 'amen.'"

—Robert L. DuPont, M.D.; author, *The Selfish Brain: Learning from Addiction*; first director of the National Institute on Drug Abuse (NIDA)

"*Dangerous Drugs* will shock readers who are indifferent to the problem of drug abuse in this country and will fill a gap in public understanding of a social problem with which the country is not yet prepared to deal."

—James Russell Wiggins, former editor of *The Washington Post*

"This is an excellent resource for parents, educators, and professionals. It provides a comprehensive overview of the nature and extent of drug abuse, summarizes the effects and consequences of the most common drugs, describes abuser characteristics and vulnerabilities, debunks myths, and discusses treatment, prevention, and policy issues, all in a straightforward and very reader-friendly style."

—Nicholas J. Kozel, Associate Director, National Institute on Drug Abuse (NIDA), Division of Epidemiology, Services, and Prevention Research

"One of the greatest defects on the war against drugs, particularly in curbing adolescent use, is misinformation. Parents and professionals must have factual information about drugs. *Dangerous Drugs* is an important resource; Carol Falkowski has performed a great service. We will expect updated editions as new substances make their appearances."

—Abraham J. Twerski, M.D.; author, *Addictive Thinking: Understanding Self-Deception*; founder and medical director emeritus, Gateway Rehabilitation Center

A HAZELDEN GUIDEBOOK

Dangerous Drugs

An Easy-to-Use Reference
for Parents and Professionals

SECOND EDITION

Carol L. Falkowski

HAZELDEN

Hazelden
Center City, Minnesota 55012–0176

1-800-328-0094
1-651-213-4590 (Fax)
www.hazelden.org

Library of Congress Cataloging-in-Publication Data

Falkowski, Carol L.
   Dangerous drugs : an easy-to-use reference for parents and
professionals / Carol Falkowski. — 2nd ed.
      p. cm. — (A Hazelden guidebook)
   Includes bibliographical references and index.
   ISBN 1-56838-981-7
   1. Substance abuse. 2. Drugs—Physiological effect. I. Title.
   II. Series.

HV4998.F35 2003
362.29—dc21   2002191313

07   6 5 4 3

Cover design by Theresa Gedig

Interior design and typesetting by Kinne Design

Interior photography by Ron Hoeschen (Banta Corporation)

Special thanks to the Minnesota Bureau of Criminal Apprehension,
Forensic Science Service Laboratory; to the Washington County
Sheriff's Office, Narcotics Unit; and to Deborah Zvosec, Ph.D.,
Department of Emergency Medicine, Hennepin County Medical
Center, and the Minneapolis Research Foundation for allowing
us to photograph at their

Contents

Contents

Contents

Figures

Preface

After finishing a presentation or media interview about drug abuse trends, I invariably hear the same comments. When the speech is over or the camera turns off, reporters and audience members alike remark, "I had no idea! I just had NO idea!!"

Two incidents in particular convinced me to write a book on drug abuse. The first happened in the 1980s when I talked on the phone to a mother who called the state alcohol and drug abuse agency requesting information about alcohol. As usual the call was routed to me.

Speaking softly and reluctantly at first, she explained that her fifteen-year-old son had just died of an alcohol overdose, "something the doctor called alcohol poisoning." His funeral had been that morning. Friends had gathered at her house afterward, and now in the late afternoon, everyone had gone home. Her husband was out, running an errand. She was alone. She was searching for more than "information."

She told me that several nights earlier, friends of her son awakened her and her husband. They were bringing her son home—drunk and unconscious. The friends readily admitted that they'd all been drinking a lot and that the son passed out. They couldn't wake him up. The parents thanked them and they left.

Together she and her husband decided it was best to let their son "sleep it off." So they put him to bed. The next morning they discovered his lifeless body in his bed, just as they had tucked him in the night before.

This grieving mother was devastated, distraught, and in a state of utter disbelief. She said, "I never knew you could *die* from drinking too much alcohol! I just didn't know! My son didn't either. Why don't they teach *that* to kids in school?" If only she'd known, she'd have warned him, she assured me. They'd never really talked about alcohol with their son, she said. And now, of course, it was too late. She seemed to be a well-educated and articulate person. She and her husband were social drinkers. Yet she did not know that drinking too much alcohol could kill you.

I remember listening to the pain in her voice and her sorrow. I remember thinking, How many other parents have walked in her shoes or will someday? How many other parents will have to endure that unbearable pain? It was one bad parental decision followed by a lifetime of blame, loss, regret, and grief.

The second incident happened in 1999, after my name appeared in a newspaper article about a relatively new drug of abuse, GHB. The wife of a man who'd recently died from a GHB overdose read the article and tracked me down because it mentioned that GHB could be addictive. It was that word, *addictive*, that caught her attention.

She wondered if her husband had been addicted to GHB. He'd used it regularly for about six months, and after a while she'd noticed he'd have to take more and more of it to feel any effect. In fact, if he didn't take any at all, his chest would "shake like an earthquake," she said.

Nothing she'd read about GHB on the Internet *ever* mentioned that it could be addictive or even harmful. "On the Internet," she said, "they make it sound like it's *good* for you." When I told her, "Not everything you read on the Internet is necessarily true, you know," there was a long pause in our conversation. This possibility hadn't quite crossed her mind before. "Really?" she said.

Ever since then I've wondered how many other people get false information about drugs over the Internet. Thousands of people, like this woman's deceased husband, purchase dangerous substances over the Internet and have them delivered right to their front door, without reading even a hint of the possible risks.

This book is written for these two women, and for everyone else who, upon learning some basic drug information, might find themselves saying, "I had no idea!"

Acknowledgments

Many people contributed to the second edition of *Dangerous Drugs*, directly and indirectly. In addition to my family, whose encouragement, patience, and support kept me going, I extend my sincere thanks to

Mike Campion, Dan Bergman, and Paul Stevens of the Minnesota Bureau of Criminal Apprehension; Pat Olson of the Washington County Sheriff's Department; Deb Zvosec of the Minneapolis Medical Research Foundation; Ron Hoeschen of Banta; and Karen Chernayev and David Spohn of the Hazelden Foundation for their role in creating these fabulous color photographs

Gregory Carlson of Hennepin Faculty Associates, Mark Groves and Dan Cain of RS Eden, Bob Olander of Hennepin County Community Services, and Maurice Rinfret of the National Drug Intelligence Center for their ongoing professional collaboration and support

Nick Kozel of the National Institute on Drug Abuse for his long-standing and contagious commitment to drug abuse epidemiology

Christine Anderson, Kris Van Hoof-Haines, Jeff Moravec, William Moyers, and Jon Zeipen of the Hazelden Foundation; and Jim Hall of UpFront Drug Information in Miami, for their promotional efforts, collegial enthusiasm, perspectives, and encouragement

Steven Setzer, R.Ph., C.S.P.I., Director of Education, Minnesota Poison Control System, Hennepin Regional Poison Center, for his expert consultation on chemistry and pharmacology

Introduction

In today's world most parents juggle jobs, day care, children's activities, and extended families. They race and rush and barely catch their breath. "Tired" is reserved for the instant before they fall asleep at night, because they spend all other waking moments running around, manically responding to the multiple demands of the family, employer, and school. And it's not just parents, by any means. It seems like everyone is increasingly rushed and short of time.

Even though drug and alcohol problems touch everyone's lives in one way or another and cost our society dearly, most people don't have the time or the inclination to learn more about them. Yes, we often read headlines about drugs and watch celebrities go in and out of rehab and jail. In election years political candidates drone on about the drug problem in America and assure us they'll get tough. Sure, people cruise the Internet or visit the library if addiction hits close to home, but other than that, their plates are full. Their time is used up. Even our educators, who arguably have a greater need to know about drug and alcohol problems, struggle professionally just to keep up with the growing daily demands of their jobs. Keeping up on drug trends seems like too much to ask.

Many of today's parents—baby boomers—came of age in the 1960s, and they now have teenagers of their own. These parents in particular may not feel the need to "keep up" on drugs. They often presume to know all about drugs because, after all, they were the hippies and the "love children" who had experiences with drugs themselves—who probably even inhaled their marijuana.

Yet when people pause for a moment to reflect on what they actually know about drugs in today's world, many come up short. Many have trouble understanding the changing nature of drug abuse in general and, in particular, the new drugs available in today's marketplace.

Drugs of abuse, how they are used, and by whom are constantly changing. Young people face increasingly dangerous choices about drugs. Advances in science promote a better understanding of the underlying mechanisms of addiction, long-term effects, and emerging treatments. Heated political posturing about drug abuse permeates modern American society. The determinants and consequences of drug abuse are incredibly costly, complex, and far reaching.

Dangerous Drugs is about the nature and extent of drug and alcohol abuse in today's society. It's not a technical, medical reference book or a physiology or pharmacology textbook. You won't read words you can find only in a medical dictionary. You won't learn about the structural areas of the brain, or what neurotransmitters are affected

To renew items:
316-733-3234 or
lwnixon@butlercc.edu

To renew Interlibrary Loan:
316-733-3351

Receipt - 11/29/2018

Butler Community College

Ransom, Shavonne A
Phone: 4055142121

Items Checked Out Today:
Dangerous drugs : an easy-to-use
reference for parents and professionals
31111201011937   Due 12/20/2018

Other Items You Have Checked Out:
The brain : what everyone needs to know
520180034   Due: 11/28/2018

nk you and have a wonderful day!

in which way by each drug, or the basics of chemistry, anatomy, or emergency medicine. Nor is this a diagnostic tool for addiction professionals, a how-to drug detection manual for employers, or a consumers guide for would-be drug abusers.

This book is about the drugs (yes, this means alcohol and nicotine, too) and other substances that are commonly abused for their mood-altering, pleasurable effects. It covers the basics about alcohol, illegal drugs, tobacco, and other substances commonly abused in the United States. The goal is to promote a better understanding of drug abuse in today's society.

The basic underlying assumption of *Dangerous Drugs* is simple: You don't need to be a medical professional or biochemist to understand the dangers of drugs and alcohol. Similarly, you don't need to understand how the flu affects the body to realize that you feel lousy when you have it. You don't need to comprehend the dynamics of flight to appreciate that an airplane crash can be fatal. And so it is with drugs. You don't need to understand chemistry or physiology to realize that drugs affect the brain in damaging ways and that abusing them is a risky, sometimes addicting, and all too often deadly proposition.

Dangerous Drugs examines how drug abuse affects all of us, not just the drug abusers. It is an easy-to-use reference book written for parents, educators, and others.

This book begins with an overview of drugs in society and ends with detailed discussions of individual drugs of abuse.

Chapter 1 surveys the landscape of current drug and alcohol abuse trends in the United States, and it answers three questions: (1) Who uses drugs? (2) What does drug abuse do to society? and (3) How does the United States currently approach the substance abuse problem, and how can prevention and treatment play a role in solutions?

Chapter 2 looks at the attraction of drug use and the economic lure of the illegal drug trade. Why do people take drugs in the first place? Why are so many drawn into the illegal drug business?

Chapter 3 discusses the signs and symptoms of abuse and dependence. How can you tell if someone is developing a drug or alcohol problem? This chapter helps you identify the behavioral signs and symptoms of a growing drug abuse problem.

Chapter 4 explains the key elements of addiction as a chronic, relapsing disease like high blood pressure, asthma, and diabetes.

Chapter 5 covers what you can do about drug and alcohol problems—both immediate and long-term. When should you call 911? What are the signs that you need to act fast and call for emergency help? How can you help a friend or a loved one who may be in trouble with drugs or alcohol? It includes a list of resources and places to go for additional help and information.

Chapter 6 discusses the unique characteristics of illicit drugs that make using them so unpredictable and dangerous, even if you aren't addicted. Illegal drugs have no safe recommended dosage or standard of purity. And they often interact in dangerous ways when used in combination with each other.

Chapters 7 to 16 focus on specific drugs of abuse and drug categories. Drugs are listed alphabetically beginning with alcohol in chapter 7 and ending with tobacco in chapter 15. Other substances of abuse, including nutritional supplements, over-the-counter cold medications, and caffeine are presented in chapter 16.

Each chapter on specific drugs of abuse presents a chart that outlines the observable indications of use, the effects of use, the duration of effects, the signs of overdose, and whether or not a fatal overdose is possible. Each of these chapters also discusses (1) the effects and consequences of use—the short- and long-term effects of using the drug; (2) the primary user groups; and (3) the recent developments—new trends in demographics, patterns of use, strength of the drug, and availability.

Dangerous Drugs is based on information and data from the U.S. Department of Health and Human Services, the Centers for Disease Control and Prevention, the National Institute on Drug Abuse (NIDA), the National Institute on Alcohol Abuse and Alcoholism (NIAAA), and others. It also incorporates conclusions and observations stemming from my many years as a drug abuse researcher.

Understanding the nature and extent of drug abuse is essential to the development and delivery of effective prevention, intervention, and treatment. Clearly there is no simple solution to the dilemma of drug abuse in today's society, yet accurate and timely information is a vital part of our understanding. Too many lives and dreams have already been shattered by drug abuse due to simple ignorance and misinformation. Considering the potential and actual devastation to individuals, families, and communities, we should all know the basic, fundamental facts about the nature and extent of drug abuse.

1. Overview of Drug and Alcohol Abuse in the United States

The abuse of dangerous drugs affects us all. The health, social, and legal consequences of their use ripple through the fabric of society. The staggering economic costs of drug and alcohol abuse are borne by individual taxpayers, small businesses, and large corporations alike. The personal costs can be devastating, sometimes fatal. Hardly a family in America hasn't been personally touched by the adverse consequences.

Primary User Groups

According to the most recent government estimates, at least 180 million people in the United States (81%) have tried alcohol at least once in their lifetime, and 87 million people (39%) have tried illegal drugs.[1]

Nearly 104 million Americans (47%) currently drink alcohol, 56 million (25%) smoke cigarettes, and about 14 million (6%) use illegal drugs. See figure 1. Among the current illegal drug users, over half (59%) use marijuana only, 17% use marijuana and some other drug, and 24% use drugs other than marijuana.

Who are the people who use alcohol and drugs? The

following section (pages 11–17) describes their basic demographic characteristics.

Mood-altering substances are more likely to be used by younger people. See figure 2. The heaviest users of alcohol, cigarettes, and illicit drugs are people between the ages of eighteen and twenty-five. Among this age group 56.8% use alcohol, 12.8% are heavy alcohol users, 38.3% smoke cigarettes, and 15.9% use illicit drugs.

Although the legal drinking age for alcohol in the United States is twenty-one, 16.4% of people age twelve through seventeen currently use alcohol. And although the laws in all fifty states prohibit the sale of tobacco to minors under age eighteen, cigarette smoking is reported by 13.4% of people age twelve through seventeen.

Men are more likely than women to use drugs, alcohol, and cigarettes. See figure 3. Illicit drug use is reported by 7.7% of males and 5% of females. Alcohol use is reported by 53.6% of males and 40.2% of females, and cigarette use by 26.9% of males and 23.1% of females.

There are also differences looking at race/ethnicity. See figure 4. Whites are more likely than people of other race/ethnicities to use alcohol (50.7%). American Indian/Native Alaskans (7.2%) are slightly more likely to report heavy alcohol use than whites (6.2%) and people of more than one race (5.2%). American Indian/Native Alaskans are most likely to smoke cigarettes (42.3%) and Asians least likely (16.5%). Illicit drug use was reported by 14.8%

of people of more than one race, 12.6% of American Indian/Native Alaskans, and 6.4% of Whites and Blacks. Asians have the lowest rate (2.7%).

Patterns of substance abuse vary by employment status. See figure 5. A greater percentage of unemployed people than employed people report cigarette use (44.2%), illicit drug use (15.4%), and heavy alcohol use (9.2%). However, because there are many more people who are employed than unemployed, the actual number of employed people who report drug and heavy alcohol use is far greater than the number of unemployed people who do so.

Among full-time workers age eighteen to forty-nine, 6.3 million (7.7%) currently use illicit drugs and 6.2 million (7.6%) are heavy alcohol users.[2] In fact, of all current illicit drug users age eighteen to forty-nine, the vast majority (70%) are employed full-time.

Patterns of alcohol, cigarette, and illicit drug use vary according to the level of educational attainment. See figure 6. For people over the age of eighteen, the greater their level of academic achievement (1) the more likely they are to use alcohol, (2) the less likely they are to be heavy alcohol users, and (3) the less likely they are to use cigarettes and illicit drugs.

Use of alcohol, cigarettes, and other drugs varies somewhat by population density. See figure 7. The biggest difference is in alcohol use, reported by 50.1% of people in large metropolitan areas and only 35.6% of those in non-urbanized, completely rural areas. Yet heavy drinking, defined as five or more drinks on the same occasion on each of five days in the past month, is most frequently reported by rural residents (6.9%), followed by residents of small metro areas (6.6%). Cigarette smoking is most prevalent in completely rural areas (27.4%) and less urbanized, nonmetro areas (27%). The lowest smoking rate is in large metro areas (23.5%) and small metro areas (25.8%). Illicit drug use is most prevalent in urbanized, nonmetro areas (6.8%), followed closely by small metro areas (6.7%) and large metro areas (6.5%). Illicit drug use is least prevalent in less urbanized, nonmetro areas (4.5%) and completely rural areas (3.9%). (See figure 7 for definitions of various population areas.)

Consequences of Substance Use, Abuse, and Addiction

Substance use, abuse, and addiction happen all around us, whether we live in the country, the suburbs, or central cities. It doesn't happen somewhere else. It happens here. It isn't somebody else's problem. It's everyone's.

We see addiction in the faces of smokers "enjoying" their cigarettes while huddled outside of office buildings or farm co-ops even in subzero temperatures. We see addiction in the posture and expression of old men lined up outside the same bar every morning, waiting for it to open at 8 A.M.

Figure 1

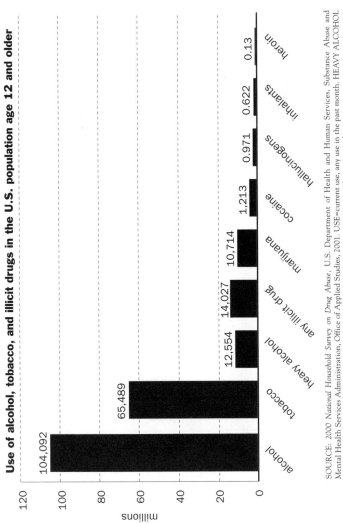

Use of alcohol, tobacco, and illicit drugs in the U.S. population age 12 and older

SOURCE: 2000 *National Household Survey on Drug Abuse*, U.S. Department of Health and Human Services, Substance Abuse and Mental Health Services Administration, Office of Applied Studies, 2001. USE=current use, any use in the past month. HEAVY ALCOHOL =drinking five or more drinks on the same occasion on each of five or more days in the past month.

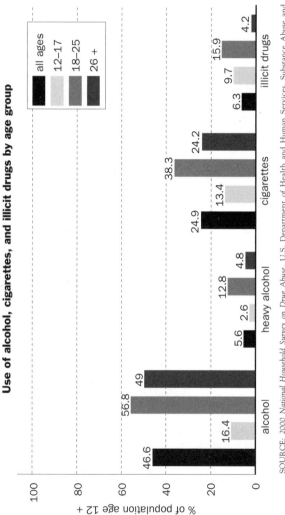

Figure 2

Use of alcohol, cigarettes, and illicit drugs by age group

Legend: all ages, 12–17, 18–25, 26 +

% of population age 12 +

alcohol: 46.6, 16.4, 56.8, 49

heavy alcohol: 5.6, 2.6, 12.8, 4.8

cigarettes: 24.9, 13.4, 38.3, 24.2

illicit drugs: 6.3, 9.7, 15.9, 4.2

SOURCE: *2000 National Household Survey on Drug Abuse*, U.S. Department of Health and Human Services, Substance Abuse and Mental Health Services Administration, Office of Applied Studies, 2001. USE=current use, any use in the past month. HEAVY ALCOHOL=drinking five or more drinks on the same occasion on each of five or more days in the past month.

12

Figure 3

Use of alcohol, cigarettes, and illicit drugs by gender

% of population age 12+

- male
- female

	male	female
alcohol	53.6	40.2
heavy alcohol	8.7	2.7
cigarettes	26.9	23.1
illicit drugs	7.7	5.0

SOURCE: *2000 National Household Survey on Drug Abuse*, U.S. Department of Health and Human Services, Substance Abuse and Mental Health Services Administration, Office of Applied Studies, 2001. USE=current use, any use in the past month. HEAVY ALCOHOL=drinking five or more drinks on the same occasion on each of five or more days in the past month.

Figure 4

Use of alcohol, cigarettes, and illicit drugs by race/ethnicity

SOURCE: *2000 National Household Survey on Drug Abuse*, U.S. Department of Health and Human Services, Substance Abuse and Mental Health Services Administration, Office of Applied Studies, 2001. USE=current use, any use in the past month. HEAVY ALCOHOL= drinking five or more drinks on the same occasion on each of five or more days in the past month. No estimate reported for Pacific Islander/Native Hawaiian use of alcohol, heavy alcohol, and cigarettes.

14

Figure 5

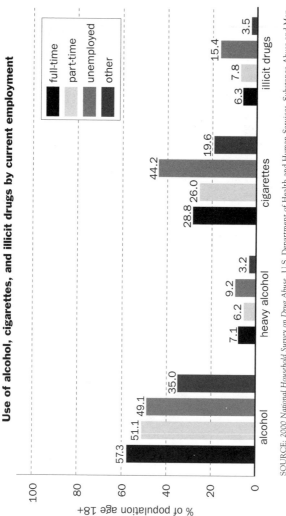

Use of alcohol, cigarettes, and illicit drugs by current employment

full-time
part-time
unemployed
other

% of population age 18+

alcohol: 57.3, 51.1, 49.1, 35.0
heavy alcohol: 7.1, 6.2, 9.2, 3.2
cigarettes: 28.8, 26.0, 44.2, 19.6
illicit drugs: 6.3, 7.8, 15.4, 3.5

SOURCE: *2000 National Household Survey on Drug Abuse*, U.S. Department of Health and Human Services, Substance Abuse and Mental Health Services Administration, Office of Applied Studies, 2001. USE=current use, any use in the past month. HEAVY ALCOHOL=drinking five or more drinks on the same occasion on each of five or more days in the past month. OTHER=student, retired, disabled, homemaker, and "other."

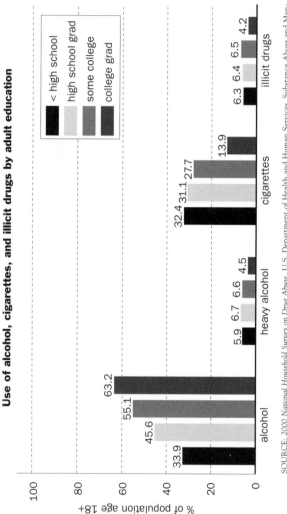

Figure 6

Use of alcohol, cigarettes, and illicit drugs by adult education

Legend: < high school, high school grad, some college, college grad

% of population age 18+

alcohol: 33.9, 45.6, 55.1, 63.2
heavy alcohol: 5.9, 6.7, 6.6, 4.5
cigarettes: 32.4, 31.1, 27.7, 13.9
illicit drugs: 6.3, 6.4, 6.5, 4.2

SOURCE: 2000 *National Household Survey on Drug Abuse*, U.S. Department of Health and Human Services, Substance Abuse and Mental Health Services Administration, Office of Applied Studies, 2001. USE=current use, any use in the past month. HEAVY ALCOHOL=drinking five or more drinks on the same occasion on each of five or more days in the past month.

Figure 7

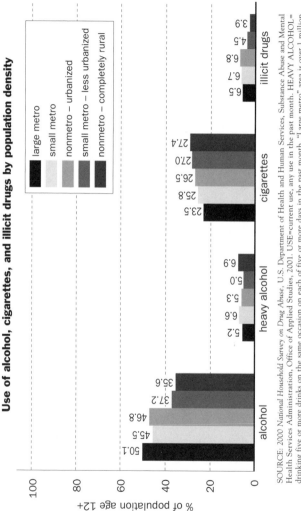

Use of alcohol, cigarettes, and illicit drugs by population density

Legend:
- large metro
- small metro
- nonmetro – urbanized
- small metro – less urbanized
- nonmetro – completely rural

% of population age 12+

alcohol
- 50.1
- 45.5
- 46.8
- 37.2
- 35.6

heavy alcohol
- 5.2
- 6.6
- 5.3
- 5.0
- 6.9

cigarettes
- 23.5
- 25.8
- 26.5
- 27.0
- 27.4

illicit drugs
- 6.5
- 6.7
- 6.8
- 4.5
- 3.9

SOURCE: *2000 National Household Survey on Drug Abuse*, U.S. Department of Health and Human Services, Substance Abuse and Mental Health Services Administration, Office of Applied Studies, 2001. USE=current use, any use in the past month. HEAVY ALCOHOL= drinking five or more drinks on the same occasion on each of five or more days in the past month. "Large metro" area is over 1 million population, "small metro" area is less than 1 million, and "nonmetro" area is any area outside of a Metropolitan Statistical Area (MSA). Within nonmetro areas, "urbanized" counties have 20,000 or more population in urbanized areas, "less urbanized" have 2,500 to 20,000 in urbanized areas, and "completely rural" have less than 2,500 in urbanized areas.

We see the harm caused by drugs and alcohol when we drive by car accidents, pull over for passing ambulances, or watch loved ones die miserably from diseases related to smoking, drugs, or alcohol. We see the pain in the lost eyes of small children who, by no fault of their own, are born into a world of addicted caregivers.

We hear the sounds of addiction in the wheezing noise of people with emphysema who struggle for every breath and in the fast double-talk of prostitutes who sell their dignity for the next hit off the crack pipe.

We sense the wild excitement and adventure of drug abuse in the giggles of young girls who say their parents would "just kill" them if they ever found out, in the bravado drinking games played in college dorm rooms, and in the nightclubs where young people exuberantly and tirelessly dance until dawn.

Many people use and abuse alcohol but do not develop alcoholism. Not every person who uses illegal drugs eventually becomes addicted. But it's not just addiction that creates what we loosely term "the drug abuse problem." It's all the factors that precede, accompany, and stem from the *use* and *abuse* of mood-altering substances. Intoxicated people, not just addicts, are hazardous to their own health and that of others. Numerous medical, public safety, public health, economic, cultural, and criminal justice problems are due to the *use* and *abuse* of mood-altering substances—not just the disease of addiction.

Too often reporters, producers, and editors try to characterize each new drug that appears on the horizon as "the most addictive" drug ever known. But in reality, using drugs and alcohol isn't dangerous just because a person might "get hooked." It's dangerous because when some people use or abuse drugs, even in the absence of addiction, the consequences to themselves and society are dire.

The consequences of use, abuse, and addiction include loss of life, physical and psychological damage, lost productivity, criminal activities associated with the illegal drug business, damage inflicted on others by users, and all the legitimate and costly social, health, and criminal justice efforts required to treat addiction and enforce the law.

Substance-Abuse-Related Mortality

Each year in the United States more than 430,000 people die from tobacco-related disease, and more than 100,000 from causes related to alcohol abuse. This compares with 16,000 drug-induced deaths annually.

Tobacco-related disease kills more Americans than alcohol, homicides, drugs, suicides, car accidents, and AIDS combined.[3] See figure 8.

Figure 8

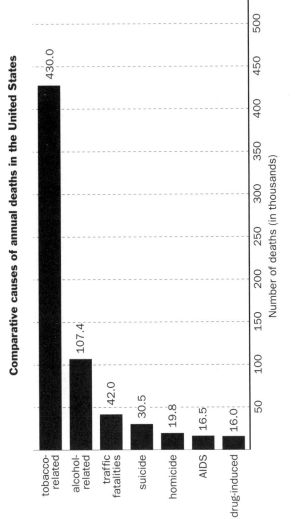

Comparative causes of annual deaths in the United States

	Number of deaths (in thousands)
tobacco-related	430.0
alcohol-related	107.4
traffic fatalities	42.0
suicide	30.5
homicide	19.8
AIDS	16.5
drug-induced	16.0

SOURCE: U.S. Department of Health and Human Services, National Institute on Alcohol Abuse and Alcoholism, and U.S. Centers for Disease Control and Prevention. (See note 1, chapter 1 for complete citation.)

Physical, Emotional, and Psychological Problems of Substance Dependence

In addition to premature death, people who abuse alcohol, tobacco, and illicit drugs experience physical, emotional, or psychological problems. Some become addicted or dependent. Of those, some receive treatment for addiction, some recover with the help of self-help groups like Alcoholics Anonymous, and some stop using with no help at all. Some people move in and out of periods of abuse, while others stay addicted for a lifetime.

The 1998 National Household Survey on Drug Abuse (NHSDA) measured the extent of the problems experienced by people who had used alcohol, cigarettes, and illicit drugs in the past year.[4] It also asked a series of questions based on the diagnostic criteria for substance dependence to help determine how many respondents could be assessed as dependent on or addicted to alcohol and illicit drugs. Finally, respondents were asked whether they had actually received help in the form of treatment or counseling.

Of the people who had used alcohol in the past year, 2.3% reported related health problems, and 4.2% reported emotional or psychological problems related to alcohol. Seven percent were assessed dependent, yet only 1.2% received some sort of treatment or counseling for alcohol.

Among people who used illegal drugs in the past year, 8.2% reported related health problems, 14.8% reported

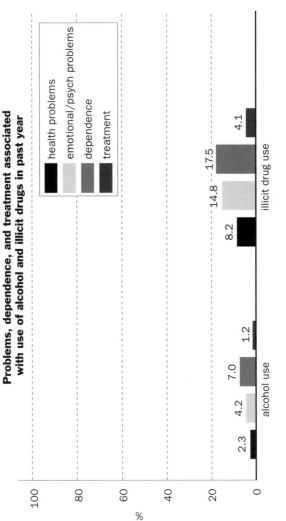

Figure 9

Problems, dependence, and treatment associated with use of alcohol and illicit drugs in past year

- health problems
- emotional/psych problems
- dependence
- treatment

alcohol use: 2.3, 4.2, 7.0, 1.2

illicit drug use: 8.2, 14.8, 17.5, 4.1

SOURCE: *1998 National Household Survey on Drug Abuse*, U.S. Department of Health and Human Services, Substance Abuse and Mental Health Services Administration, Office of Applied Studies, 1999. Annual averages based on 1997 and 1998 data. USE=any use in the past year. Sma 99-3328 tables 53b and 51b.

emotional or psychological problems, 17.5% were assessed dependent, and 4.1% received some sort of treatment or counseling. See figure 9.

A larger proportion of illicit drug users than alcohol users experienced physical, emotional, or psychological problems, were assessed dependent, and received treatment. Of those who were dependent on either alcohol or drugs, however, very few received treatment or counseling. For alcoholics, only 17% received treatment, and for illicit drug addicts, only 23% of those who needed it received treatment or counseling.

Risks of Infectious Disease

People who abuse drugs and alcohol also place themselves at increased risk for contracting other diseases. They tend to have compromised overall health status, which substantially lowers their resistance to infection. Addicts, for example, do not typically engage in health-promotion activities or value a balanced diet, plenty of sleep, and exercise. Because of this, they are at heightened risk for contracting communicable, infectious diseases such as HIV (AIDS), hepatitis, tuberculosis, and sexually transmitted diseases (STDs). And once infected, they are more likely than nonusers to progress to serious illness and death due to lack of access to or noncompliance with treatment.

Estimated Numbers of Past Year Alcohol and Drug Users Reporting Problems, Dependence, and Treatment

REPORTED PROBLEMS	ALCOHOL USERS	ILLICIT DRUG USERS
Physical problems	3.2 million	1.9 million
Emotional/psycho-logical problems	5.8 million	3.5 million
Dependence	9.7 million	4.1 million
Received treatment/counseling	1.7 million	963,000

SOURCE: *1998 National Household Survey on Drug Abuse*, U.S. Department of Health and Human Services, Substance Abuse and Mental Health Services Administration, Office of Applied Studies, 1999. Annual averages based on 1997 and 1998 data. USE=any use in the past year.

By sharing contaminated injection drug equipment or having sexual contact with someone who is already infected, a person risks blood-borne transmission of HIV or hepatitis. Roughly one-third of the cumulative AIDS cases in the United States diagnosed through June 2000 (789,472) were related to injection drug use. Heterosexual contact with an injection drug user is a major source of HIV infection among women.[5] HIV infection can also be spread by non-injection drug abusers who trade sex for drugs, engage in unprotected sex while under the influence, or use drugs in other ways that can facilitate transmission, such as intranasal bleeding while snorting drugs or by blood-borne exposure to lesions on the mouth and lips related to smoking crack cocaine.

Almost four million Americans are infected with hepatitis C virus (HCV), a blood-borne liver disease. It is already endemic within some addicted populations.[6] Injection drug use accounts for most cases of HCV in the United States. Like other blood-borne pathogens, the virus is contracted through the transfer of infected blood via shared syringes or by way of other infected injection equipment. HCV is acquired more rapidly after introduction to injection drug use than hepatitis B or HIV. Hence, among new initiates to injection drug use, the rate of HCV exceeds that of HIV. Among young injection drug users, rates of HCV are four times that of HIV.[7]

Unlike many STDs whose symptoms appear relatively shortly after exposure, HCV attacks the liver and can quietly damage the organ and its vital functions for up to two decades before obvious symptoms or illnesses emerge. That means many people diagnosed with HCV actually contracted the virus many years before and have only recently started showing symptoms. Most injection drug users contract HCV early on in their drug abuse activities. One recent study of people who had been injecting drugs for six years or less found an HCV prevalence rate of 77% and a hepatitis B rate of 66%.[8]

Drug-induced impaired judgment can result in unwanted sexual activity, particularly among adolescents. The results can be sexually transmitted diseases or pregnancy or both. The National Center on Addiction and

Substance Abuse found that adolescents who drink were much more likely to engage in sex, at younger ages, and with multiple sex partners.[9] Another survey of high school students found that 39% of boys and 18% of girls thought it was acceptable for a boy to force sex on a girl if the girl was drunk or stoned.[10]

Half of all adolescents are sexually active by age seventeen. The highest rates of gonorrhea, syphilis, and pelvic inflammatory disease are found among sexually active adolescents. One-quarter of these adolescents will contract an STD before leaving high school.[11] Each year roughly three million cases of sexually transmitted disease and one million pregnancies occur among teenagers.[12]

Tuberculosis (TB) is an airborne bacterial disease most prevalent in areas with crowded, substandard living and health conditions. In the United States, the risk of contracting TB is two to six times greater among drug users than nonusers. In 1996, an estimated 11% of new TB cases were among drug users.[13]

What are the consequences and implications of these heightened risks of infectious disease among drug abusers? Because the treatment of these infectious diseases typically involves complicated, long-term periods of medication and doctor visits, adherence to these regimens is particularly challenging for chronic drug abusers and addicts. While some do comply, a larger percentage does not. Since finishing the entire course of treatment is a requirement of effective disease control, the non-compliance of this infected population precipitates a growing risk of resistant viral and bacterial strains that are not treatable by existing medications and could result in new, emerging epidemics.

Substance-Abuse-Related Fetal Effects

Substance use during pregnancy is harmful to the developing fetus and child. It can result in permanent physical and developmental problems for the newborn and child. Children harmed by their mothers' drug use during pregnancy often need expensive care, such as neonatal intensive care and surgical units; ongoing medical, psychological, and learning services; and, in extreme cases, residential and institutional services.

In 1992, the National Institute on Drug Abuse conducted a national survey among 2,613 women delivering babies in fifty-two urban and rural hospitals to determine the extent of prenatal exposure to substances of abuse.[14]

The rates of substance use during pregnancy were as follows: 20.4% smoked cigarettes, 18.8% drank alcohol, 5.5% reported illegal drug use, 2.9% marijuana use, and 1.1% cocaine use. In 1992, more than four million women gave birth in the United States, so the number of newborns prenatally exposed was substantial.

The effects of using substances during pregnancy depend on the drug. Smoking during pregnancy reduces the amount of oxygen available to the developing fetus. It also creates a higher risk of spontaneous abortion early in the pregnancy, lower birth weight, and premature delivery.[15]

Reported Maternal Substance Use during Pregnancy

	PERCENT	ESTIMATED NUMBER
Smoked cigarettes	20.4%	819,700
Drank alcohol	18.8%	756,900
Used illegal drugs	5.5%	220,900
Used marijuana	2.9%	118,700
Used cocaine	1.1%	45,100

SOURCE: *National Pregnancy and Health Survey—Drug Use Among Women Delivering Livebirths: 1992*, U.S. Department of Health and Human Services, National Institutes of Health, National Institute on Drug Abuse, 1996. NIH publication no. 96–3819.

Alcohol use by a pregnant woman can produce birth defects, the most serious being fetal alcohol syndrome (FAS). FAS, first identified in 1973, describes patterns of physical abnormalities as well as permanent developmental, behavioral, and mental problems found in children of alcoholic mothers. An estimated 1 to 3 of every 1,000 babies born have FAS.[16] A growing body of evidence suggests that drinking even moderate levels of alcohol during pregnancy can produce growth, cognitive, and behavioral problems, although less severe than those among children with FAS.[17] For this reason, the best course is to avoid all alcohol use during pregnancy, according to the

National Institute on Alcohol Abuse and Alcoholism.[18]

Prenatal exposure to cocaine, marijuana, or opiates increases the risk of premature birth, smaller head circumference, and lower birth weight and height. Prenatal exposure to other illicit drugs is harmful, too, but less well studied.

The effects of illegal drug use during pregnancy are difficult to study because so many women who use illegal drugs also use alcohol and cigarettes, and may also have other conditions that negatively affect a developing fetus, such as poor nutrition and general health. Many addicted mothers have poor parenting skills, have low maternal interest, and often live in chaotic home environments. These factors can also negatively affect child development and mother-child bonding.

Animal studies, however, by eliminating some of these confounding effects, show that prenatal cocaine exposure affects the areas of the brain related to attention and learning. Coupled with the results of other studies conducted with children prenatally exposed to drugs, these studies seem to indicate that prenatal drug exposure impairs the child's ability to regulate emotional states (stress, frustration) and maintain focused attention on tasks. Both of these factors, in turn, impair the child's ability to learn.[19]

Health Care Utilization Related to Substance Abuse

Alcoholics and people who use cigarettes and illicit drugs compromise their health status. Because of this, and the acute ill effects of the drugs themselves, they utilize health care services at a substantially higher rate than nonusers. It's estimated that 25% of all Americans in general hospital beds (not including maternity or intensive care units) are being treated for complications of alcoholism.[20] In addition, in 2000 in the United States, more than 601,000 episodes in hospital emergency departments involved drugs.[21] Many chronic drug abusers and addicts lack health insurance coverage as well.

Family Problems Related to Substance Abuse

Drug and alcohol abuse and addiction are family problems, whether the addict or abuser is a parent, a child, or an extended family member. In a 1999 national Gallup Poll, 36% of respondents reported that drinking alcohol had been a cause of trouble in their families in the year of the survey, the highest rate since the question was first asked in 1947.[22] One out of four children grows up in an alcoholic family, according to a 1999 study by the National Institute on Alcohol Abuse and Alcoholism. This represents nineteen million children, or about 29% of all children under age eighteen.[23]

Growing up in an alcoholic home can affect a child's cognitive and emotional development in negative, sometimes long-lasting ways. Not only are biological children of alcoholics at increased genetic risk of developing alcoholism, but all children who grow up in alcoholic families are at higher risk of serious disruption in their family lives. Family instability, in turn, places them at increased risk of developing problems with cognitive functioning, academics, emotional distress, and behavior.[24]

Lost Productivity

Among full-time workers age eighteen to forty-nine, 6.3 million (7.7%) are current illicit drug users, 6.2 million (7.6%) are heavy alcohol users, and 1.6 million (1.9%) are both. This exacts a toll in terms of lost productivity due to substance use, abuse, or addiction. People under the influence or dealing with the associated psychological and social instability of the abusing lifestyle are not fully contributing employees. Heavy alcohol and drug users are more likely than others to work for multiple employers, leave their jobs voluntarily, and skip days of work.[25]

Crime and Criminal Justice

Alcohol and drug abuse are criminal justice problems of enormous magnitude. Because mood-altering chemicals impair judgment, people under the influence become more inclined to do things they might not ordinarily do, behaviors that may place them at risk not only for disease but for social deviance as well. Simply put, drug users are more likely than nonusers to commit crimes.

Many people commit crimes while under the influence of drugs and alcohol. Because so many people drink alcohol and so many people drive cars, alcohol-impaired driving is the most common.

Alcohol and drug use are associated with a wide range of other criminal activities as well. In fact, roughly half of state inmates and a third of federal inmates were under the influence of drugs or alcohol when they committed their crimes, according to a report by the Bureau of Justice Statistics. Over 80% of state and 70% of federal prisoners reported past drug use.[26]

Some people commit crime to finance their personal addiction. In the same study of inmates, one out of six reported committing their current offense to obtain money for buying drugs. The cost of sustaining a heavy heroin or cocaine habit, for example, can be hundreds of dollars per day, and addicts look to crime as a way to maintain that level of cash flow.

Other people, not necessarily drug users, produce, sell, or traffic in illegal drugs strictly as a lucrative business. In 1997, 20% of state and 60% of federal inmates were imprisoned for a drug law violation.[27] The use of alcohol, and to a lesser degree illegal drugs, is established in most assaults, homicides, manslaughters, and attempted homicides and many property crimes, rapes, and robberies. Alcohol and drug abuse are often involved in cases of child abuse and neglect.[28] One research study of violent offenders found that up to 57% of men and 27% of women involved in marital violence were drinking at the time of the offense.[29]

The National Institute of Justice, through its ongoing Arrestee Drug Abuse Monitoring (ADAM) program, routinely tests newly arrested people in jails in more than thirty cities nationwide. The arrestees are interviewed by researchers, and a urine sample is obtained within hours of their arrest. People arrested for all types of crime are included, not just drug offenders. In 2001, male arrestees who tested positive for at least one drug ranged from 51% in Des Moines to 79% in New York City.[30]

Economic Cost of Substance Abuse and Addiction

The total economic cost of drug abuse in the United States is enormous, an estimated $143.4 billion in 1998 alone. Of this, 69% was attributable to lost productivity, 22% to other effects, and 9% to health care costs.[31] See page 34.

The Office of National Drug Control Policy estimated that in 2000, American drug consumers spent $64 billion on the purchase of cocaine, heroin, marijuana, methamphetamine, and other drugs but contended that these expenditures were less than the societal costs associated with drug consumption: drug-abuse-related criminal justice, catastrophic and long-term health care, addiction treatment, and prevention programs.[32]

The Economic Cost of Drug Abuse in the United States, 1998

COST CATEGORY	% OF TOTAL	DOLLAR AMOUNT (IN MILLIONS)
PRODUCTIVITY LOSSES	**69%**	**$98,465**
Incarceration		30,133
Crime Careers		24,627
Drug-Abuse-Related Illness		23,143
Premature Death		16,611
Productivity Loss—Crime Victims		2,165
Institutionalization/Hospitalization		1,786
COSTS of OTHER EFFECTS	**22%**	**$32,082**
Criminal Justice/Other Public Costs (police protection; legal adjudication; local, state, and federal corrections; federal spending to reduce supply)		31,099
Private Costs (private legal defense, property damage for crime victims)		734
Social Welfare		249
HEALTH CARE COSTS	**9%**	**$12,862**
Medical Consequences (hospital and ambulatory care, drug-exposed infants, TB, HIV/AIDS, HCV, health insurance administration, crime victim health care)		5,721
Community-Based Specialty Treatment		4,933
Federally Provided Specialty Treatment (Department of Veteran Affairs, Department of Defense, Indian Health Service, Bureau of Prisons)		474
Support (Local, state, and federal prevention, prevention research, training, treatment research, insurance administration)		1,734
TOTAL COST (in actual dollars)		**$143.4** billion

SOURCE: Office of National Drug Control Policy, *The Economic Costs of Drug Abuse in the United States, 1992 –1998*, Publication no. NCJ-190636 (Washington, D.C.: Office of the President, 2001).

Recent Trends in Drug Abuse

Problems related to substance abuse and addiction are pervasive, expensive, painful, and long-standing. The range of issues related to drug and alcohol abuse is difficult to grasp and even harder to measure. The enormity, complexity, and interrelatedness of substance abuse issues also make charting progress problematic at best. People who are in successful recovery from addiction remain, for the most part, a silent constituency, which makes estimates about their number imprecise. Regarding drug availability and misinformation, the Internet has made both more accessible, which broadens the reach, thus raising the risks.

Also, the apparent inability of politicians to resist the "drug war" sound bites gets in the way of seeing the entire picture with clarity. Reducing this complex issue to "get tough on crime" rhetoric serves no one. Moreover, the divisive national debate on drug policy slows the development of a consensus on what constitutes "success" and "progress." As a nation we are becoming increasingly polarized on the issues, yet almost everyone concedes that prevention and treatment are inextricable parts of any long-term solution.

Recovery Success Stories: The Hidden Population

The social stigma associated with being an alcoholic or an addict can often linger, even if the person hasn't used drugs or had a drop to drink for twenty years. At times the stigma prevents people who are "clean and sober" from ever publicly identifying themselves as being in recovery from the disease. Even after years of being sober, successful, contributing citizens, employees, and family members, many who are living in recovery from addiction never publicly identify themselves as such.

Consequently, there is no organized, highly visible constituency of people who have, in essence, survived addiction. There are politically active cancer survivor groups and MS survivor groups, for example, but none for recovering addicts and alcoholics. Therefore, unlike groups that rally and advocate for increased funding for other diseases, such as breast cancer, birth defects, or AIDS, recovering alcoholics and addicts have no single political voice. In part because of this, government funding for treatment and research is not commensurate with the magnitude of the problem.

The Internet Effect

The exact nature and extent of drug abuse is also difficult to measure due to advances in electronic commerce and communication. The Internet has been a great equalizer of information and misinformation about drugs, bridging any possible preexisting knowledge gap between city and rural residents, for example. Facts about drugs and alcohol are now more accessible than ever. But at the same time, the Internet also provides an instant source of misinformation about the effects of drugs and alcohol.

Web sites promote the benefits of substance abuse or present one-sided, misleading, and inaccurate information. On-line chat rooms direct users to the latest rave party in their area or let them tell others about their recent drug experience or party. People can purchase substances promoted as beneficial to their health, only to discover serious adverse effects with use. Drug abusers can post the latest scores from their favorite drinking game, compare home recipes for the illegal manufacture of drugs, or simply find fellowship among other drug abusers—twenty-four hours a day. This flood of information and misinformation heightens the risks and creates confusion about the actual dangers of drug and alcohol abuse.

To underscore the sheer magnitude of this problem, consider some basic Internet facts. In 2000, an estimated 85% of Americans age twelve through twenty-four used the Internet regularly, compared with 59% of adults age twenty-five and above. An estimated thirty million adolescents under the age of eighteen currently use the Internet, with forty million expected by 2005. According to the National Drug Intelligence Center, "The threat to adolescents and young adults in the United States accessing the Internet consists of information, disseminated by drug offenders or others, that is intended to facilitate the production, use, or sale of federally scheduled nonprescription drugs."[33]

The Internet sale and distribution of nonscheduled, unregulated substances is an equally dangerous and growing threat as well. An increasing number of elusive, short-lived Web sites tout "research drugs" (drugs to be used for research purposes only), as veiled attempts to legitimize the activity. Some even go so far as to have purchasers sign disclaimers that the drugs are not intended for human consumption and will be used for research purposes only. Some label the products as "experimental raw material," for example. The often hallucinogenic, highly concentrated substances are typically identified by short acronyms that represent very long chemical names, such as 2C-T-7. They are pills or powders or liquids. In terms of chemical structure, many are "designer drugs," chemical compounds that are just a molecule or two away from scheduled, controlled substances, as yet another strategy to evade prosecution.

Internet-facilitated prescription drug sales are another area of considerable growth and concern. To obtain drugs that require a doctor's prescription, some Web sites ask a few on-line medical questions and claim that a doctor reviews the responses before a prescription is mailed out. Other sites ask only for credit card information and a mailing address. Some foreign-based Web sites specialize in selling pharmaceutical drugs that require a prescription in the United States but not in the host country.

The Unending Political Posturing on Drug Abuse

The drug abuse problem provides great rhetorical posturing opportunities for politicians. Ever since former President Richard Nixon declared a "war on drugs" during the Vietnam "conflict," this cliché has arguably done more harm than good. If we are fighting a war, are addicts the enemy? Aren't they people with a disease? And what about drunk drivers or cigarette smokers? Smoking kills more people than alcohol and illegal drugs combined. Are we fighting the disease or the people who have it? Or are the enemies just the people who supply the drug? In that case, what about the manufacturers and distributors of legal drugs such as alcohol and tobacco? By making enemies out of people addicted to drugs, the war on drugs has deepened the stigma and impeded progress toward more effective prevention and treatment.

Yet invariably the drug war metaphor lives on. Despite the growing evidence that some current strategies need serious adjustment, politicians at all levels of government regularly renew the "war on drugs" battle cry, especially during election years.

Harm Reduction

Harm reduction describes an approach to drug policy in which the primary goal is improving public health by reducing the harm caused both to the user and to society.[34] On the surface, this sounds logical. But what does the term really mean in practice?

It may seem, for instance, that most aspects of the current approach to substance abuse reduce harm. Law enforcement officers, after all, reduce harm by protecting the public safety. When police arrest drunk drivers, they prevent accidents and fatalities. They stop at least some drug trafficking and illegal drug sales, which in turn reduces harm. In addition, society reduces harm by trying to prevent people from using drugs in the first place. Drug and alcohol treatment reduces harm by giving addicts and alcoholics the tools they need to recover from their addictions and rejoin society in healthy, responsible ways. All of these efforts reduce the harm that comes from drug abuse and addiction, right?

The phrase *harm reduction*, as it is used today, however, means something else, something much more specific. The harm reduction approach accepts that some people will keep using drugs. It presumes, therefore, that the best approach to the drug and alcohol problem is to lessen the damage by providing users with the means to do it in a less risky, more healthy manner.

An early application of the harm reduction approach in the United States came in the late 1980s with syringe-exchange programs aimed at reducing the spread of AIDS among injection drug users. The idea was to let addicts exchange dirty, used syringes for sterile ones at no cost and thus slow the blood-borne transmission of HIV through the sharing of contaminated syringes. The widespread fear that this would result in new injection drug users proved unfounded, and HIV rates among syringe exchangers declined or held constant. The programs were seen as a huge success: they reduced the harm of injection drug use to both the addict and society. Nonetheless, federal funds still may not be used for syringe-exchange programs.[35]

Another example of harm reduction was the distribution of informational flyers at raves in San Francisco in the 1990s. These flyers provided tips on how to use Ecstasy (an illegal stimulant drug with mild hallucinogenic properties) safely and without bad side effects by resting occasionally and drinking lots of liquids.

The evolving harm reduction school of drug policy has not only challenged conventional thinking but also polarized discussions about how best to approach the problem of drug abuse in America. We don't quite all agree about what to do next.

In one camp are the "prohibitionists" and "drug warriors" who, at the very least, want to continue current public policy approaches that include a blend of interdiction, law enforcement, prevention, and treatment. They believe legalization is bad public policy that will increase drug abuse problems.[36] They point out that one legal drug, tobacco, is far and away the biggest threat to public health and that our other legal drug, alcohol, is the biggest threat to public safety. Adding to the list of legal drugs, they argue, would only increase the social burden.

In the other camp are "harm reductionists" and "legal-izers" who, at the very least, support an across-the-board shift from seeing drug and alcohol abuse as a criminal justice problem to seeing it as a public health issue. At the very extreme, however, some would have us believe that the *only* harm that comes from using drugs is a result of their illegal status. Harm reductionists often point out that prohibition of alcohol didn't work. They often advocate for voter referendums on decriminalization of marijuana, or they develop drug education courses that emphasize responsible use instead of drug resistance skills or abstinence.

And some privately financed drug abuse policy insti-tutes specialize in distributing pro–drug abuse literature in every possible venue.

Future Solutions

Looking to the future, two approaches to the drug abuse problem seem clear and advisable: effective, available treatment for addiction and more enlightened, broader-based drug and alcohol abuse prevention.

Addiction Treatment and Recovery

Some people recover from addiction without formal treatment in medical settings. The largest self-help group for alcoholics is Alcoholics Anonymous (AA); Narcotics Anonymous and other drug-specific groups also exist and operate on the same AA principles. Worldwide, an estimated 97,000 AA support groups help people achieve or maintain sobriety. The only requirement for AA membership is the desire to stop drinking. Because of the stigma of alcoholism and the anonymity of these groups, however, it is virtually impossible to estimate with precision the number of people who have successfully recovered from addiction using Twelve Step or other programs.

Fortunately, addiction is a treatable disease. In 1999, there were 1.6 million admissions to substance abuse treatment programs in the United States. Of those, 46.5% had a primary alcohol diagnosis, and 53.5% had primary drug diagnosis. Of these treatment settings, 64% were ambulatory admissions, 18% residential or rehabilitation, and 18% twenty-four-hour detoxification services.[37]

Treatment for addiction produces outcomes similar to those in the treatment for other chronic diseases such as diabetes, asthma, and high blood pressure.[38] Successful treatment does more than simply interrupt the use of mood-altering substances. People learn to handle daily life and negotiate major challenges without using mood-altering substances. Providing treatment for addiction increases productivity and employability and restores the broken lives of individuals and families.

Treatment is also a cost-effective approach. It saves money over time because it reduces the future social, health, and criminal justice costs associated with addiction. In one of the most comprehensive research studies of its kind, the California Department of Alcohol and Drug Programs showed that each dollar spent on drug and alcohol treatment saved seven dollars in future crime and health care costs.[39]

In spite of this, health care benefits for addiction treatment are eroding. Too often addiction treatment benefits are limited under managed health care packages. Current trends in public and private health care packages often "carve out" addiction treatment funding. Most people don't realize, unless it hits close to home, that even with a full-time job that carries a "decent" health care insurance plan, chances are slim that the entire cost of addiction treatment will be covered by insurance. With this push toward such limited benefits for addiction treatment, many worry that effective treatment, especially for the poor, will become less available.[40]

This is particularly unfortunate because untreated addiction incurs much larger social welfare, criminal justice, and health care bills. Consider that incarcerating an adult costs up to $37,000 annually, whereas treatment for addiction costs an average of $14,600 for residential or $2,300 for outpatient services.[41]

Drug and Alcohol Abuse Prevention

Substance abuse prevention is in the best public interest and can save money and lives. Delaying the age of first alcohol and drug use reduces the likelihood of developing drug and alcohol problems for a lifetime. Studies have shown that the earlier the age of first use, the more likely the development of future problems and addiction.[42] That is why delaying the age of first use is an important goal of prevention.

The other major goal of prevention is to reduce known risk factors and promote protective factors among youth. Numerous research studies have identified factors at the individual and community level that place adolescents at increased risk for developing drug and alcohol problems, as well as protective factors that may reduce the risk. These factors are summarized in the tables on page 46.

Too often, drug and alcohol abuse prevention is relegated to a single classroom activity for children in grade school and consists of little or nothing beyond that. We tend to see prevention as exclusively a school responsibility and ignore the fact that parents, peers, the community, and the media have equally important roles to play.

Risk Factors

- chaotic home environment
- parental substance abuse or mental illness
- ineffective parenting, especially with children with difficult temperaments and conduct disorders
- lack of mutual attachment and nurturing
- inappropriate shy or aggressive behavior in the classroom
- failure in school performance
- poor social coping skills
- affiliations with deviant peers or peers around deviant behaviors
- perceived peer, school, family, or community approval of drug-using behaviors

Protective Factors

- strong bonds with family
- parental engagement in child's life
- clear parental expectations and consequences
- success in school performance
- strong bonds with positive social institutions (school, community, faith-based organizations)
- adoption of conventional norms about drug and alcohol use

SOURCE: *Preventing Drug Use Among Children and Adolescents: A Research-Based Guide*, U.S. Department of Health and Human Services, National Institutes of Health, National Institute on Drug Abuse, 1997. NIH publication no. 97–4212.

Parents, in particular, grossly underestimate the important influence they can have on their children's decisions about drugs. In a 1996 nationwide survey of parents, almost half (40%) said they had little or no influence on their children's decision to use drugs.[43] Yet parents can play a critical part in prevention by being role models, by staying involved and engaged in their children's lives, and by communicating expectations about their children's academic achievement and conduct. But many parents remain so unclear about when and how to talk with their children about drugs and alcohol that they say nothing at all. This is unfortunate, because from the child's perspective, parental silence can translate into implicit approval of drug and alcohol abuse.

Many parents seem to operate under the illusion that when their child reaches a certain age, it's time for "the drug talk." Instead, parents need to point out the dangers of drug and alcohol use all along the way. Just as they tell a young child not to accept candy from strangers and to look both ways before crossing the street, they need to offer drug and alcohol messages that fit with the age of the child. The key is to match the amount of information with the context of the child's questions and the child's maturity level. There are numerous situations where drug and alcohol topics arise in the course of daily life—with the morning newspaper, TV commercials, billboards, or the nightly news. Parents need to take advantage of those opportunities to give their children clear messages in a natural, spontaneous way.

Studies have found that children who know what their parents expect of them and have clear limits are less likely to engage in all sorts of high-risk behaviors, including drug and alcohol abuse. It's up to parents to voice their expectations and establish consequences *before* risky situations arise. And above all, parents need to stay connected with their kids' lives, even when it may seem impossible.

"I think when the D.A.R.E. officers show you
all the drugs it just makes you want to use them more.
Some of the stories they tell make it look really cool."

— a seventh-grade D.A.R.E. student and
D.A.R.E essay winner in fifth grade

But what about schools and the community? Invariably, when community leaders are asked what is being done about drug and alcohol prevention, they answer, "We have D.A.R.E." And too often that's the end of the conversation. Drug Abuse Resistance Education (D.A.R.E.), a course taught by law enforcement officers to fifth graders about what drugs are and how to resist peer pressure to use them, is probably the most popular drug education class in the country. Yet it achieves minimal long-term results in preventing future drug abuse.[44]

This inability to produce long-term results may be due, in part, to the paucity of other prevention efforts that reinforce the classroom activities. Too often school-based programs are offered in only one grade level and operate in a community-wide vacuum.

Drug and alcohol abuse prevention must be more than a classroom activity for fifth graders. In the absence of the reinforcing, deliberate involvement of the community at large, the lasting effects of *any* school-based prevention class may be negligible, whether the class is about buckling up seat belts, brushing teeth, eating nutritious foods, or avoiding drugs.

Many parents think prevention is the school's job. And the schools think prevention is the parent's job. And community businesses and churches tend to assume that prevention is certainly not *their* job. But it is.

In short, effective drug and alcohol prevention involves the same message delivered by different messengers. Effective prevention efforts require the active involvement of not just schools, but also parents, extended families, businesses, faith-based organizations, and students themselves—in other words, entire communities.[45] Even though the research is quite clear about this, most communities have yet to seriously step up to the plate regarding drug and alcohol abuse prevention.

2. Why Drugs?

The Attraction and Harm of Alcohol and Drug Abuse

Why do people get involved in drugs in the first place? What makes drug and alcohol abuse so attractive? Why do some kids develop problems and others don't? What leads people into the business of illegal drugs?

The Attraction of Substance Abuse

What's the motivation for initial use of drugs and alcohol? In the simplest of terms, the reason is straightforward and easily understood. People use drugs and alcohol to feel good. That's it. The motivation to use drugs may stem from sensation or thrill seeking, or be a form of self-medication born out of a desire to escape an unpleasant reality or haunting memory. But whatever the reason, the end result is the same: Drugs make you feel good. They make you feel better, at least temporarily.

Drugs operate via the pathways of the brain and affect what is known as the reward center. Billions of nerve cells in the brain chemically and electronically communicate and define experiences as pleasurable or rewarding. The more pleasurable something is, the more we want to repeat it. Sex and eating are naturally rewarding, and so we like to repeat those experiences. It is similar with drugs and alcohol.

Every category of drug that is abused for its pleasure-producing properties affects these electronic circuits of the brain in one way or another. Recent scientific and technological advances have broadened our understanding of these processes enormously. Drugs work at multiple brain sites through multiple actions. Some drugs accelerate the body's production of certain brain chemicals that make a person feel good. Other drugs keep the brain from moving the chemicals on through the brain, thus prolonging the pleasurable sensations. Other drugs damage the brain's structure, perhaps permanently, so that the feelings of pleasure can never again be fully experienced.

Everyone likes to feel good, including adolescents. As part of their natural development into adulthood, they engage in a variety of new activities and behaviors. They explore the world around them. In this modern age, they needn't look far to encounter opportunities to use drugs and alcohol. The opportunities present themselves to children at younger and younger ages. Half of eighth graders and nine out of ten twelfth graders report that marijuana is easy to get. Three-quarters of eighth graders say the same about alcohol and cigarettes.[1]

Trying drugs and alcohol is a way for them to feel good or better. It can be a self-medicating or a thrill-seeking behavior. Teenagers are drawn to mood-altering substances out of curiosity. They also know it's the forbidden fruit, and for some teens drug, alcohol, or tobacco use is also a convenient way to be naughty, deviant, and rebellious.

Adolescents often feel invulnerable to harm. In spite of whatever factual information they may have received, they tend to minimize any harmful effects of drug and alcohol use. Adolescents tend to live in the present; the long-term effects of drug use, and diseases such as lung cancer or cirrhosis of the liver, don't seem to apply to them. Such consequences are as remote and irrelevant as gray hair, retirement investment plans, or hip replacement surgery.

Like it or not, some experimentation with drugs and alcohol is virtually inevitable. The good news is that while many adolescents will try drugs and alcohol, most will not develop serious problems with them.

A great deal of research has attempted to identify factors that place a child at heightened risk for problems with drugs and alcohol. And while entire books have been written on the topic, here are the basics.

What can increase risk of an adolescent developing a drug or alcohol problem?

- early age of first use
- feeling unloved by family, low mutual attachment with parents, ineffective parenting

- chaotic home environment
- poor social coping skills
- perceived external approval of drug use (by peers, family, community)
- affiliation with deviant peers
- working at a job or having above-average disposable income
- past or current drug or alcohol problems within the family
- past or current family emotional or physical abuse or neglect
- past or current sexual abuse

What can reduce the risk of an adolescent developing a drug or alcohol problem (in addition to the absence of the above conditions)?

- feeling connected with and valued by family and other significant adults
- parental supervision and involvement with child's activities
- high educational aspirations of parents and child
- academic success
- feeling connected with school and valuing academic achievement

- strong bonds with social institutions (school, community, church)
- personal disapproval of drug and alcohol use
- personal belief that drug and alcohol use is dangerous and harmful
- having parents who verbalize expectations about and consequences for using alcohol or other drugs

The reasons one child develops a serious problem with drugs or alcohol and another child does not are multi-faceted and numerous. They have been the subject of considerable scientific inquiry.[2] The preceding lists simply highlight, in a very general way, factors known to increase and reduce risk. There are more.

The Economic Lure of the Illegal Drug Business

Without a supply of drugs, users could not sustain their habits. Huge, almost unimaginable profits are made from the sale and trafficking of illegal drugs, both domestically and internationally. Profits are reaped at every step along the distribution chain, from production to distribution to wholesale to retail. Every entrepreneur along the way roughly doubles his or her initial investment by passing on to the next buyer a more diluted product in smaller packaged amounts.

Mexico, for example, is both a source country for illegal drugs and a pathway into the United States for drugs produced elsewhere. The United States shares a two-thousand-mile border with Mexico that has thirty-nine border crossings. The volume of legitimate traffic across this border is staggering. In 1996, for example, 3.5 million commercial trucks and railroad boxcars arrived in the United States from Mexico, and 254 million individuals legally crossed into the United States from Mexico.[3] Sheer numbers make the detection of illegal drugs at the border akin to finding a needle in a haystack, in spite of increasingly sophisticated methods of detection and greater and greater staffing devoted to the effort.

From sophisticated criminal organizations to desperately impoverished individuals working alone, people are drawn to the drug trade by the prospect of big money in the lucrative U.S. drug market. Take, for example, a family man living in a small Mexican border town, working and struggling on annual earnings of $350. He's asked to drive a car across the border and up to Chicago. He's instructed to park the car on a certain block of a certain street, leave the keys under the floor mat, and then take a bus back home. For this he's offered $300.

He accepts the job and is handed a map, car keys, gas money, a bus ticket, and instructions on how to avert suspicion when crossing the border. Does he realize there are illegal drugs hidden in the car? Probably. Does he ask?

Probably not. Assuming he doesn't get caught, will he do it again? Who's to say? But this is not simply a story; it's an everyday occurrence.

In the late 1980s, in certain U.S. urban centers, young boys were increasingly recruited as drug couriers and lookouts. If they were apprehended, business would not be seriously disrupted, and the penalties for minors are less severe than for adults. For a young boy living in poverty, it's hard to pass up the chance of earning $50 or $100 or even $10 per hour for something as simple as being a lookout for the cops by riding your bicycle around the block and keeping your eyes open.

In rural areas, the plight of the family farm is well documented. The net profit on the sale of one acre of corn is about $50. The sale of one large plant of high-potency marijuana can bring a net profit of $1,000. And who knows better than farmers about how to make plants grow?

Or imagine an elderly, retired manual laborer, barely making ends meet, living just above the poverty level on a fixed income. He worked hard all his life, paid taxes, and avoided welfare. He has chronic, debilitating pain due to a lifetime of injury from his backbreaking work. Fortunately, his condition can be effectively treated by prescription pain medication, which, taken as directed, allows him to live a more "normal," pain-free life. Then one day he realizes that he can resell his prescription medication in the illicit drug market for ten times the amount it cost him at the pharmacy.

So whether a person is an otherwise honest, hard-working farmer, a blue- or white-collar worker with an indoor marijuana growing operation, an impoverished city boy, or a migrant farmworker, the profits from illegal drugs are there for the taking. Anyone who is willing to take the risk can realize the profits. For some skilled wage earners, the drug trade provides supplemental income. For other people, it can represent an economic opportunity that would not otherwise exist. Some might even consider the drug trade their only realistic opportunity for financial gain. And this brief discussion only scratches the surface of the many issues related to the economics of illegal drug sales.

3. Signs and Symptoms of a Drug or Alcohol Problem

As a person progresses from substance use to abuse and possibly dependence, there are observable behavioral signs and symptoms.

Generally speaking, the more often a person turns to drugs or alcohol in response to an uncomfortable life situation, the greater the likelihood of an impending abuse problem. For example, you may notice a person saying, "I need a drink" in response to more and more situations. The list of life situations where this is true typically grows longer as a person progresses from abuse to dependence.

A marked increase in the amount of drug a person consumes and the frequency of use can also be observed as dependence develops and progresses. This is because physical tolerance often accompanies addiction, which means that the body requires an increasing amount of the drug in order to achieve the desired effect. So a noticeable increase in both the amount consumed and the frequency of use can signal a growing abuse or dependence problem.

But addiction is more than just repeated, heavy drug or alcohol use. Compulsive use and loss of control are hallmarks of addiction, which means that a person can no longer use in moderation. Addicts can no longer control when to stop using. They use to the point of intoxication virtually every time.

A noticeable shift in attitudes and interests also occurs with chronic abuse and addiction. Gradually the user's priorities start to change. Activities and interests that were once important fall to the wayside, replaced by an unending interest in the drug. People who are addicted develop a strong craving for the drug or drug-induced state, becoming almost completely preoccupied with thoughts about the drug.

As a parent, you may notice a drop in your teen's academic performance, a change in peer group, more secretive behavior, mood swings, and increased defensiveness when queried about activities or whereabouts. Because even teens who don't use alcohol or other drugs exhibit some of these behaviors during the normal course of adolescent development, identifying drug problems among teens is especially challenging.

A parent's desire to believe that his or her child does *not* have a drug abuse problem can also be problematic. For example, when parents concerned about changes in their adolescent's behavior sit the child down to explore the possibility of drug abuse, the child will most often respond quickly with, "Oh Mom (or Dad), you know I would *never* do drugs!" And rather than acknowledge that adolescents are seldom inclined to readily admit any wrongdoing to parental figures (whether about drugs or anything else), the parents will rush to their own relief by their child's denial. And too often the topic will never be broached again.

The fact of the matter is that parents seldom readily accept wrongdoing by their child, and children seldom readily admit any wrongdoing to their parents. And *that* is why it is so important to get a professional chemical dependency assessment of a child when drugs or alcohol may be involved. Adolescents may initially be more forthcoming about their substance abuse with someone *other* than their own parent.

Addiction is not a single, immediate event, but rather a gradual process. So the more you notice the above changes starting to happen, the greater the likelihood that an addiction may be developing. Simply put, a person is addicted when the acquisition and use of drugs and alcohol continue to be the primary focus of daily life, even in the face of the personal, family, social, employment, or legal problems that it creates. For an addict, the drug is the focus around which all else revolves.

Yet because the addictive process is gradual and because personal relationships with the abuser often cloud an objective assessment, the progression is not always noticeable or recognized for what it is. Herein lies the problem.

Certain physiological symptoms of intoxication and chronic use are drug specific and will be discussed in the later chapters of this book. Many of the behavioral signs of a drug or alcohol problem, however, can be generalized across all drug categories.

Signs of substance abuse include the following:

- always uses to intoxication
- uses at inappropriate times, such as before driving, at work, or at school
- misses work or school due to using
- damages relationships at school, work, or home due to use

The following behavioral clues can also signal a growing substance abuse problem:

- stealing or borrowing money from work, home, or friends
- secretive behavior about activities and possessions
- defensiveness about one's whereabouts
- unusual mood changes
- abrupt temper outbursts
- changes in eating or sleeping habits
- a change in peer group
- decreasing job or school performance or punctuality
- deterioration in personal appearance or hygiene
- loss of interest in usual activities, pastimes, and hobbies

Substance abuse can be characterized as a pattern in which a person fails to meet personal obligations and starts getting into trouble because of the chronic abuse of drugs. Alcohol and drug abuse, unlike dependence, do not involve strong craving, loss of control, or physical tolerance.

The National Institute on Alcohol Abuse and Alcoholism recommends you ask the following questions to help identify a growing alcohol problem.[1] One "yes" answer suggests an alcohol problem, and two "yes" answers means an alcohol problem is highly likely. (To make it easy to remember, it's called the **CAGE** test, for the first letters of the key words in each question.)

- Have you ever felt you should **CUT DOWN** on your drinking?

- Have people **ANNOYED** you by criticizing your drinking?

- Have you ever felt bad or **GUILTY** about your drinking?

- Have you ever had a drink the first thing in the morning (an **EYE OPENER**) to steady your nerves or to get rid of a hangover?

According to the American Psychiatric Association, abuse is defined as follows:[2]

Substance Abuse Criteria

"A maladaptive pattern of substance use leading to clinically significant impairment or distress," in conjunction with one or more of the following occurring within a twelve-month period:

1. recurrent use results in failure to meet obligations at school, work, or home

2. recurrent use in physically dangerous situations

3. recurrent legal problems due to use

4. continued use despite recurrent social and interpersonal problems due to use

SOURCE: *Diagnostic and Statistical Manual of Mental Disorders*, 4th ed. (DSM-IV), American Psychiatric Association (Washington, D.C.: APA, 1994), 182.

---

4. What Is Addiction?

Because drugs alter the functioning of the chemical pathways of the brain, they can artificially create pleasurable states and feelings like those we get naturally from food and sex. It's not inherently harmful to feel good. But the problem with getting there artificially via mood-altering substances lies in the accompanying risks of negative health and behavioral effects, both immediate and long-term.

It is important to realize that drugs and alcohol are dangerous not just because they are addictive, but also because they have immediate, short-term negative effects on a person's health and mental functioning.

Altered brain chemistry produced by drugs and alcohol impairs judgment, memory, learning, cognition, and decision-making capabilities. People under the influence of mood-altering chemicals do things they might not ordinarily do. They aren't thinking clearly—it's that simple. Because of their impaired judgment and reduced mental capacity while under the influence, people may inadvertently find themselves in dangerous situations and be unable to escape.

Impaired physical functioning also leads to accidents and injury. Reaction time is slowed. Perception of speed, sight, and sound is changed. People get clumsy. They fall down. They get hurt.

Many trauma cases treated at hospital emergency rooms are the result of drug- or alcohol-induced accidental injuries. Alcohol plays a role in nonfatal motor vehicle injuries, fires and burns, hypothermia and frostbite cases, other accidental injuries, and suicides.[1] Drug and alcohol concentrations can also reach such high levels in the body that a person dies from toxicity or poisoning, cardiac arrest, respiratory arrest, or stroke.

In addition to these short-term, potentially fatal effects, the long-term abuse of drugs and alcohol can also damage organs. It can result in serious chronic diseases such as lung cancer from smoking, liver disease from chronic heavy drinking, or addiction itself.

Again, addiction is more than just using many drugs for a long period of time. It is a disease.[2] It is a chronic, relapsing disease that requires lifelong management and periodic medical services. Why one person becomes addicted and another does not is influenced by the interaction between

1. the user—individual genetics, biology, personality, age of onset of use, expectations, and psychological state;

2. the drug itself—characteristics including potency and type of drug and the route of administration; and

3. the environment—the social setting, the group expectations, the cultural context.

In the early twentieth century alcoholism was viewed as a moral failing. In the 1950s, the American Medical Association defined addiction as a disease. We now realize that addiction is *not* a moral failing, a weakness of character, or willful misconduct. Even though people initially choose to use alcohol or drugs, once addicted they cannot control the use; the choice is replaced by compulsive drug-seeking behavior. The inability to control one's use, among other things, is what distinguishes *abuse* from *addiction*.

Addiction is a lifelong condition that must constantly be negotiated. As with other chronic diseases, such as high blood pressure (hypertension), diabetes, or asthma, addiction does not disappear even when the symptoms subside. Like other diseases, addiction has a biological, molecular basis and a predictable course and outcome. It is a progressive disease; if left untreated, it will get worse.

Alcoholics do not know with the first drink whether they will develop alcoholism, any more than children eating their first french fries know whether they will someday develop high blood pressure. Although many addicts say that they knew they were hooked the first time they used, such statements are subjective personal analyses rather than scientific findings.

Like patients with other chronic diseases that include behavioral components, addicts do not always comply with the prescribed treatment regimen and typically require more than one treatment.[3] Treatment doesn't always work on the first attempt. People may not immediately change their behavior in a way that's most beneficial to living with the disease.

The return to drug use for an addict is known as *relapse,* which is why addiction is known as a relapsing disease. But when people living with diabetes, asthma, or high blood pressure become symptomatic and require additional medical intervention, this is called "noncompliance with treatment," not relapse. And while we don't typically regard an insulin-dependent diabetic who has an occasional piece of candy as a "treatment failure," that is often the case when an alcoholic returns, however briefly, to drinking.

Politicians and others often decry the effectiveness of addiction treatment, claiming that it doesn't work simply because people need it more than once. In fact, the course of treatment for addiction is very similar to that of other chronic diseases. So while addiction *is* indeed a chronic, relapsing disease, its treatment is regarded differently from other chronic illnesses such as diabetes, high blood pressure, and asthma.

How many people suffer from addiction to alcohol? In 1992, 4% of U.S. adults age eighteen and older met the standard diagnostic criteria for alcohol dependence, and 3% met the criteria for alcohol abuse, according to the National Longitudinal Alcohol Epidemiologic Survey.[4]

The America Psychiatric Association generally defines addiction, or substance dependence, as follows:[5]

Substance Dependence Criteria

A group of cognitive, behavioral, and physiological symptoms that result in continued self-administered use of a substance despite major substance-related problems, characterized by tolerance, withdrawal, and compulsive drug-taking behaviors. Three or more of the following occurring in the same twelve-month period:

1. tolerance

2. withdrawal

3. use in larger amounts than intended

4. desire or unsuccessful attempts to restrict use or cut down

5. spending a lot of time obtaining the substance

6. decline or elimination of significant social, occupational, and recreational activities due to use

7. continued use in spite of known physical or psychological problems due to use

SOURCE: *Diagnostic and Statistical Manual of Mental Disorders*, 4th ed. (DSM-IV), American Psychiatric Association (Washington, D.C.: APA, 1994), 181.

For an addict, life centers on the drug; everything else is secondary. Addicts develop a complete preoccupation with locating, administering, and recovering from the use of the drug. They dedicate most of their time to drug-seeking and drug-taking behavior. The substance becomes the major focus of their lives, and all other obligations, relationships, and activities take a backseat.

A key feature of addiction is tolerance. Tolerance is present when the body requires a greater amount of the substance over time in order to achieve the desired effect. Law enforcement officers often see the effects of alcohol tolerance when measuring the blood alcohol concentration (BAC) levels of impaired drivers. A drinker with a tolerance for alcohol, for example, could be driving a vehicle with a BAC of 0.30%, while a drinker without tolerance would typically be unconscious at that high a BAC.

"Just because some people use drugs doesn't mean they are 'bad' people. They just have a problem."

— a fifteen-year-old girl

Withdrawal is the physiological state of distress induced by the sudden absence of a substance in the tissue or blood of a longtime heavy drug or alcohol user with tolerance. But neither withdrawal nor tolerance is a necessary component of a dependence diagnosis.[6] Addicts typically try to maintain a certain level of the drug in their systems to avoid the discomfort of withdrawal. The withdrawal effects are usually the opposite of intoxication effects, can be severe, and in extreme cases can precipitate other health problems.

Other hallmarks of addiction include the inability to control use and a compulsive, intense craving for the drug. Even after the drug use stops, the craving can continue for a long period of time. Many ex-smokers report a lifelong craving for nicotine.

While brain chemistry generally resumes normal functioning levels once the drugs have been removed (the exact amount of time required for this reversal varies by drug), prolonged drug use and addiction can alter the brain functioning and possibly even the brain structure in longer-lasting ways. With the advent of brain-scan-imaging technology, significant scientific discoveries have advanced the understanding of addiction as a brain disease with environmental, physiological, and social aspects.[7]

5. What to Do about a Drug or Alcohol Problem

Drugs and alcohol produce both immediate, harmful health effects and more gradual, long-term consequences. This prompts two important questions for people whose loved ones use drugs or alcohol: (1) Confronted with an immediate, potentially critical situation involving drugs and alcohol, when do you call 911? (2) When it is *not* a medical emergency, how do you help a person who is in trouble with alcohol or drugs regain control of his or her life?

When to Call 911

Although later chapters discuss the effects of specific drugs in detail, there is one overriding consideration that applies across all drug categories:

Drug and alcohol use kills people.

Many people die accidentally from the complications caused by consuming excessive amounts of drugs and alcohol or by encountering unanticipated potency, adulterants, and drug interactions. Others die because their impaired judgment landed them in life-threatening situations. People *do* die, and what begins as a fun adventure can turn sour in an instant. The immediate consequences of drug and alcohol abuse can be permanently disabling or fatal, so do not hesitate to call for emergency medical help. Minutes can make the difference between recovery, disability, and death.

If you are confronted with a person who is unconscious due to the use of drugs or alcohol, your best course is to call 911 and seek emergency medical treatment immediately.

After you have called 911, if the person is conscious, you may want to ask what he or she took and try to get as much detailed information as possible, such as how much and how long ago. You may also want to search the area and person for any possible clues about what substances were ingested, such as drug paraphernalia, bottles of prescription drugs, or packets of illegal drugs. It is important to share information or evidence you discover with emergency medical personnel so that their medical care is based on as much information as possible.

How to Help Someone with a Drug or Alcohol Problem

Fortunately we live in a country where help is available for people with drug and alcohol problems. Whether your first call for help is to your health care provider, a social service agency, or a self-help group like Al-Anon or Alcoholics Anonymous, help is available. Addiction *is* a treatable disease.

Communication, however difficult, is the first step in addressing a substance abuse problem and getting help for someone. If you are willing to talk with the individual abusing drugs or alcohol, here are some tips:

- Don't confront a person about his or her use while the person is high or drunk. Wait until later when the effects of the drug have completely abated.

- Expect to be put on the defensive. A person with a substance abuse problem will vehemently deny having one. The person may lash out at *you* and try to convince you that only *you* have a problem.

- State your intentions—that you are confronting the person out of caring and concern, not blame or judgment. You intend to be helpful and assist the person in regaining control over his or her life.

- State your motivation—that you are having the conversation, however difficult, because you care about him or her and what happens to him or her. If you didn't care, you wouldn't bring it up.

- Be firm in your presentation. Persist in trying to make the person realize that the situation is out of control. Come prepared with specific examples of out-of-control behavior.

- Present your observations of the person's behavior.

Focus on what you see happening to the person and the lives of those around him or her. Be very specific.

- Express how the person's behavior makes you feel. Articulate your feelings clearly.

- State why you think the person needs help in stopping the addiction. Many other people have recovered from addiction and gone on to lead successful lives. Getting well and staying well often require the help of others.

- State what you will do next. This could include assisting the person in getting help as well as involving other significant people in the person's life in an intervention.

Few addicts and alcoholics readily accept that they have a problem, much less that they need an intervention or treatment. It is, therefore, extremely important if you are the primary significant person in the addict's life that you do not rely on the abuser or addict to make the contacts to get the help he or she needs. Act as you would if your loved one had any other medical condition that left him or her incapable of getting help alone.

If you are unable or unwilling to openly discuss the issue with the abuser, you can call on professionals who can assist and advise you. No matter how impossible a situation may appear, appropriate help from qualified professionals *is* available. Seek professional help! Your first stop could be your health care provider or, depending on the circumstance, a local crisis hot line, an employee assistance program, or a community social service agency. The point is that help *is* available regardless of where you live.

If you are an adolescent or young person who wants to get help for a friend or a family member, go to a trusted adult who you think can help, or contact the social worker at your school as your very first step.

Here are some resources for getting help that can start you off in the right direction.

Helpful Phone Numbers

Center for Substance Abuse Treatment Toll-Free Referral Helpline
800-662-HELP

Hazelden Foundation
800-257-7800

National Clearinghouse for Alcohol and Drug Information
800-729-6686

Helpful Web Sites

The Official Alcoholics Anonymous World Services Web Site
www.alcoholics-anonymous.org

Cocaine Anonymous World Services

www.ca.org

Hazelden Foundation

www.hazelden.org

Marijuana Anonymous World Services

www.marijuana-anonymous.org

Narcotics Anonymous World Services

www.na.org

Nicotine Anonymous

www.nicotine-anonymous.org

Prescription Abuse

www.prescriptionabuse.org

Recoveries Anonymous: The Solution-Focused Twelve Step Fellowship

www.r-a.org

Substance Abuse Treatment Facility Locator

www.findtreatment.samhsa.gov

Drug and Alcohol Information

Columbia University's Health Question and Answer Internet Service

www.goaskalice.columbia.edu

What to Do

Community Anti-Drug Coalitions of America

www.cadca.org

Hazelden Foundation

www.hazelden.org

National Clearinghouse for Alcohol and Drug Information

www.health.org

National Institute on Alcohol Abuse and Alcoholism

www.niaaa.nih.gov

National Institute on Drug Abuse

www.drugabuse.gov

Partnership for a Drug-Free America

www.drugfreeamerica.org

Project GHB

www.projectghb.org

Substance-Abuse-Related Public Policy Issues

www.jointogether.org

6. Important Considerations about Illicit Drug Use

The following chapters describe drugs that are commonly abused, particularly by young people. Not *every* drug—illegal, legal, prescription, or over-the-counter—is included, just the most common drugs of abuse. This book presents the most current information on what they are, how they affect people, who uses them, and recent developments about their use.

Nonmedical use of prescription drugs, while an area of growing concern and magnitude, is also not addressed in great detail. Significant and possibly life-threatening risks accompany prescription drugs when they are used in a manner other than medically directed. It can be extremely dangerous to take prescription medications in combination with alcohol or certain other medications (illegal, prescribed, or over-the-counter) or in an amount exceeding the recommended dose. The results are unpredictable.

There's a risk that a book like this could be used as a how-to manual for people who want to experiment with alcohol and other drugs. Therefore, the specific brand names of medications, solvents, and other products used as drugs of abuse, and those used in manufacturing illicit drugs, are intentionally omitted.

Bear in mind that the effects of drug consumption on any given individual vary according to the physical and psychological characteristics of the user, the type and strength of the drug, and the setting in which it is used.

The onset and duration of effects are influenced by

- the amount ingested
- the rate of ingestion
- the route of administration (oral, smoked, snorted, injected)
- the weight, age, and gender of the user
- preexisting health conditions of the user
- the physical tolerance of the user
- the expectations of the user—what someone is led to believe will happen and how those effects are defined by the user and the people around him or her as adverse or pleasurable
- other substances (such as over-the-counter or prescription medications, nutritional supplements, or illegal drugs) and foods that have been ingested

In addition, there are other challenges and considerations when generalizing about the effects of both legal and illicit drugs. With alcohol, for example, what is the desired effect? What is "appropriate use"? Is it defined behaviorally or by a certain blood alcohol level? The answer varies not only with the individual, but also across society at large. And the answer to whether there can be any appropriate use of illegal drugs depends on whom you ask.

The bottom line with the use of illegal drugs is this: Because they are manufactured in various unknown, uncontrolled, often makeshift conditions, users *never* know with any amount of certainty exactly what they are getting. Many ingredients unknown to the user could have been part of the original process or added along the way. How can users be sure what a drug will do if they don't even know what it is? Whenever people use illicit drugs, they're taking an enormous chance.

Route of Administration

The more rewarding a drug is to the brain, the more likely that the user's brain will want to repeat the experience. How quickly the drug reaches the brain plays a major role in producing the initial rush, or euphoria, and in determining how rewarding the brain finds it.[1] The more slowly a drug enters the brain, the less intense the initial euphoria. And the quicker the initial euphoria, the more rewarding it is, and the more the brain wants to repeat the experience.

The point is this: Drugs that are smoked and injected reach the brain the fastest, so the effects are felt sooner. The stronger the reward associated with a drug, the greater its potential for abuse, because the brain craves a repeat performance.

Take crack cocaine, for example. Although white powder cocaine was available for many years, not until cocaine was smoked (in the form of crack cocaine) did it become a widespread epidemiological phenomenon. Crack cocaine prompted a tremendous growth in the number of new cocaine users. It delivered the drug to the brain very rapidly, intensifying the initial rush. Thus, once crack became available, smoking cocaine soon replaced snorting as the main route of cocaine administration, and crack became a more widespread drug of abuse than snorted cocaine ever was.

No Standard Dosage Unit

Prescription medications have a therapeutic range within which the drug will have the desired beneficial effect. If the dose is too little, there is no effect, and if it is too great, there is a harmful effect. To achieve the therapeutic dose, the doctor considers the age, weight, and health status of the patient. Needless to say, none of this occurs with illicit drugs. Drug dealers are neither inclined nor qualified to make such recommendations, and so street drugs have no standard, recommended dose.

For example, with illicit drugs such as GHB that are sold and consumed in liquid form, the user's standard dosage may be a swig from the bottle. But what constitutes a swig, sip, or gulp varies considerably. Is a swig bigger than a sip but smaller than a gulp? And for whom?

Similarly, when a person puts a knockout type of drug such as Rohypnol or other "date-rape" drugs in a woman's beverage without her knowledge, what is the dose? And how does that vary depending on whether or not the beverage also contains alcohol? Generally speaking, the greater the dose of the drug, the greater the response. But with illegal drugs, even the desired response is open to interpretation.

Because there are no standard, uniform dosages, it is very difficult to describe with 100% certainty the specific effects of illegal drugs.

No Standard Purity Level

When you use a prescription medication, you know exactly how many milligrams of the active ingredient are contained in each pill. With illicit drugs there's no such guarantee. Street drugs are typically combined with other substances, and as a result, some drug samples contain more pure drug than others. Users can never tell by the naked eye if their particular sample of drug is of high or low purity.

Government-operated crime labs analyze street drugs seized by law enforcement agencies to determine, first, if they are actually controlled substances. They also analyze the sample to determine how much pure drug is present. For example, a white powder alleged to be cocaine, upon lab analysis, may turn out to contain only 30% pure cocaine. The remaining white powders are known as *cuts* or *adulterants*. Sugars, anesthetics, and laxatives are sometimes found as cuts in cocaine, for example.

At each level of drug dealing, sellers usually "step on" the drug. This means they add more adulterants to increase the amount of finished product, so they can make more profit. By the time a drug travels through the hands of multiple dealers, the purity level, or amount of actual active drug, can be quite low.

Sometimes a user who is accustomed to ingesting a drug of a certain consistent (although unknown) strength inadvertently buys a drug of greater purity. Even experienced heroin addicts cannot determine the purity level of a substance sold to them simply as heroin by looking or tasting. So, for example, if an addict encounters a batch that contains 60% pure heroin instead of 20%, even though he or she may inject the same amount of the drug mixture as yesterday, the addict can die from an overdose because this new batch contains much more pure heroin. Unanticipated variations of drug purity often result in overdose deaths, especially with injectable narcotics.

Another issue related to purity is that adulterants, by-products, and contaminants found in illicit drugs can sometimes themselves produce allergic or other adverse reactions. Illicit drugs are not produced in sterile conditions by large pharmaceutical companies. They often contain contaminants that are accidentally or intentionally added. Some illicit drugs contain by-products that were created in the homemade manufacture of the drug and were not entirely removed before the drug was sold. These things may happen when labs are moved quickly for fear of being discovered by law enforcement. One type of homemade methamphetamine, for example, was pale green and known for making the user vomit violently. The color came from the residue of a gun-cleaning chemical, one of the ingredients used in making the drug.

Some adulterants occur naturally, such as molds and fungi that grow on plants used as illegal drugs of abuse. Marijuana plants, for example, are often grown in a warm climate, harvested, and perhaps hung out to dry a bit. They are then compressed, wrapped in dark plastic, concealed in a cramped space, and transported across long distances. Once the marijuana reaches its final destination, the buyers open the large bags and divide the marijuana brick into smaller packages for further wholesale distribution or eventual retail sale.

At each step along the way, contaminants can be introduced, from bacteria on the hands of handlers to other substances that are spilled on the marijuana during repackaging or shipment. In addition, the shipping conditions foster the growth of molds and fungi, which tend to flourish on any damp plant material that is contained in a dark, warm, airtight environment. The fungi and molds, in turn, can be sources of illness or infection to users, particularly those whose health status is already compromised.

Drugs Used in Combination

It is rare for a substance abuser or an addict to use just one drug at a time. The most obvious example is a bar or tavern filled with cigarette smoke. Smokers are more likely to be drinkers; heavy drinkers are more likely to be smokers. It's common for marijuana smokers to simultaneously drink alcohol and for users of all types of illegal drugs to also use alcohol, tobacco, and marijuana.[2]

Substance abusers tend to take drugs in combination. Some are legal drugs, some are prescription medications, some are illegal drugs, and some are over-the-counter products. Experienced opiate addicts, for example, often abuse antianxiety prescription drugs, because of the way their effects combine with the effects of the opiates.

But combinations of multiple substances, whether taken accidentally or intentionally, can sometimes produce unwanted and unintended effects. Drug interaction occurs when the effects of one drug combine with effects of another drug or drugs, and this places the user at risk for serious adverse health consequences.

Some drugs, like alcohol and narcotics, slow down digestion, which in turn slows the absorption of other drugs. Some drugs hasten the excretion of other drugs, while some—like monoamine oxidase inhibitors (MAOIs) and decongestants—combine with certain foods, alcohol, or amphetamines to raise the blood pressure to dangerously high levels. Simultaneously taking two central nervous system depressant drugs, like alcohol and narcotics, can produce *potentiating effects*. This means that the effects of the two drugs together are even greater than the effects of each single drug added together. This is potentially fatal. Sedative/hypnotic drugs combined with alcohol can produce coma. And because alcohol lowers blood sugar, it can create complications for people already taking certain types of medications.[3]

7. Alcohol

Observable Indications of Use	Slurred speech Unsteady gait Loud voice Impaired motor control or clumsiness Flushed face Smell of alcohol on breath
Effects of Use	Feelings of intoxication Sensory alteration Anxiety reduction Possible increased heart rate
Duration of Effects	Dose dependent, variable
Signs of Overdose	Vomiting Confusion Unconsciousness Shallow breathing Convulsions Shock
Fatal Overdose Possible	Yes, due to respiratory arrest or aspiration of vomit, causing suffocation **IMPORTANT: If you suspect a person may have overdosed on alcohol, your best course is to call 911 and seek emergency medical treatment immediately.**

Alcohol, a central nervous system depressant, is also known as liquor, booze, juice, or sauce. It is a liquid obtained by fermentation of carbohydrates by yeast or by distillation.

Types of Alcohol

Ethanol (ethyl alcohol) is beverage alcohol. **Isopropyl alcohol** is rubbing alcohol, used as a disinfectant, and **methyl alcohol** is wood alcohol, which is used in cooking fuel.

Ethyl alcohol is ingested orally in beverages that are sold legally in the United States to individuals at least twenty-one years old. There are many slang terms for alcohol intoxication, including *drunk, hammered, sloshed, lit, tanked,* or *smashed.*

The major types of alcoholic beverages are distilled spirits, beer, and wine. A standard drink, or dosage unit of alcohol, generally consists of one and a half ounces of 80-proof distilled spirits, one twelve-ounce bottle of beer or wine cooler, or one five-ounce glass of wine. All three contain roughly the same amount of absolute alcohol: one-half ounce. According to the National Institute on Alcohol Abuse and Alcoholism, moderate alcohol use—up to two drinks per day for men and one for the elderly and women—is not considered harmful.[1]

Effects and Consequences of Use

Alcohol has been described as a "social lubricant" in that it may lower interpersonal inhibitions and anxiety. After ingesting moderate amounts, the user may appear flushed as small blood vessels dilate just beneath the skin. A person under the influence of larger amounts of alcohol usually exhibits an unsteady gait, blurred vision, and slurred speech. Vomiting may precede loss of consciousness. Alcohol poisoning is possible and can be fatal. Memory lapses during prolonged bouts of heavy drinking, known as blackouts, can also occur. During a blackout, the drinker is functioning, conscious, and alert, yet once the alcohol has passed through the system, he or she does not recall events or experiences that transpired.[2]

Chronic alcohol abuse results in organ damage. The determinants of alcoholism and other alcohol-related diseases are complex. Preexisting factors such as genetic vulnerability and other health conditions can affect

---

"The first time I got really drunk when I was young, I went to the wrong place at the wrong time and I wound up getting raped. Looking back at it now, some thirty years later, I was so naive and inexperienced to begin with. The alcohol only made me dumber and so much more vulnerable to harm. I've wished every day since that it had never happened."

— a middle-aged woman, social drinker

someone's likelihood of developing a disease related to alcohol use. The major disorders that may result from chronic drinking include liver diseases, pancreatitis, brain damage (organic brain disorders and reduced cognitive functioning), heart disease, and vascular disorders (hypertension, stroke).[3] Chronic drinking also increases the risk of developing certain cancers, including cancers of the esophagus, pharynx, and mouth. There is a less conclusive association with breast, liver, and colorectal cancers.[4]

People under the influence of alcohol have diminished coordination, judgment, reaction time, and motor skills. Because both drinking alcohol and driving motor vehicles are so prevalent, people driving under the influence of alcohol represent a serious and widespread threat to the public safety, and a substantial number of motor vehicle crashes involve alcohol. About three out of ten Americans will be involved in an alcohol-related car crash at some point in their lives.[5] An average of one person every two minutes is injured in an alcohol-related crash (310,000 people in 2000).[6] In that same year, there were 16,653 alcohol-related traffic fatalities—an average of one alcohol-related traffic fatality every thirty-two minutes.[7]

Criminal and administrative laws prohibit driving after drinking specified levels of alcohol, and roughly 1.5 million drivers were arrested for driving under the influence of alcohol or narcotics in 1999.[8] Blood alcohol concentration (BAC) measures the weight of alcohol per volume of blood to determine the amount of alcohol in a person's body. BAC measurement developed as a tool for law enforcement to determine the degree of impairment a person exhibits when driving after drinking. The higher the BAC level, the greater the level of impairment.

"On the way home from a baseball game after drinking beer all afternoon in the sun, I drove my truck down a city sidewalk. The passengers who were with me told me about it later, but I had no clear memory of it at all, only a vague recollection of driving very close to buildings. My God! I could have killed somebody, and I wouldn't have even realized it!"

— a former alcohol abuser, recalling a blackout

For many years, most states had a legal limit for adults of 0.10% BAC, although impaired driving skills can occur with a BAC as low as 0.02%. A healthy 160-pound man drinking two twelve-ounce beers on an empty stomach can reach a BAC of 0.04% in one hour.[9] In October 2000 the United States Congress enacted legislation setting .08% BAC as the national standard for impaired driving. States that do not enact .08% laws by 2004 face losing 2% of certain federal highway construction funds, with the penalty increasing to 8% by 2007.[10] At least thirty-four states had .08% impaired driving laws as of November 2002.

Because young people tend to be less experienced than older people in both drinking and driving, they represent a heightened threat when driving after drinking alcohol. Since 1998, all fifty states have had "zero tolerance laws" or "not a drop laws," where the legal BAC level for drivers under the age of twenty-one is between 0.00% and 0.02% (depending on the state).[11]

Primary User Groups

Alcohol is the most widely used drug in the United States, with an estimated 104 million current users in 2000—about 47% of the total population over age twelve.[12] Alcohol use is most common among people between the ages of eighteen and thirty-four, followed by those thirty-five and older, and lowest among twelve- through seventeen-year-olds. (Current use is defined as any use in the past thirty days.)

Binge alcohol use is defined as having five or more drinks on the same occasion at least once in the past thirty days. An estimated 46.4 million Americans (20.6% of the population age twelve and older) were current binge alcohol drinkers in 2000, or 44% of all drinkers. Young people age eighteen to twenty-five are the most likely to binge drink; 37.8% report it.[13]

Heavy drinking is defined as having five or more drinks on the same occasion on five or more days in the past month. It is also most common among people age eighteen to twenty-five; 12.8% in this group report heavy drinking.[14]

In 2000 one in ten Americans reported driving a motor vehicle under the influence of alcohol at least once in the previous year. Yet among young adults age eighteen to twenty-five, nearly one out of five (19.9%) reported doing so.[15]

Because the legal drinking age is twenty-one in all fifty states, the rate of alcohol use among underage people is astounding. (See figures 10 and 11.) In 2001, 80% of high school seniors, 70% of tenth graders, and 50.5% of eighth graders reported using alcohol at least once in their lifetime. Current alcohol use was reported by half of high school seniors, 40% of tenth graders, and 21.5% of eighth graders. Sixty-four percent of high school seniors had been drunk, one-third in the past thirty days.[16] Most students thought it was "fairly easy" or "very easy" to get alcohol.[17]

About half of all admissions to addiction treatment programs in 1999 were for alcohol (46.5%), compared with 59% in 1992. Overall, 26% were for alcohol only,

"My D.A.R.E. officer told us that drinking beer is okay, just as long as we don't drive afterwards."

— a fifth-grade D.A.R.E. graduate

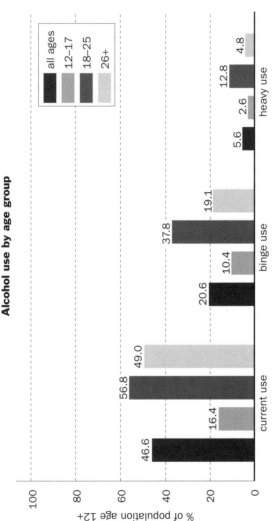

Figure 10

Alcohol use by age group

Legend: all ages, 12–17, 18–25, 26+

% of population age 12+

current use: 46.6, 16.4, 56.8, 49.0

binge use: 20.6, 10.4, 37.8, 19.1

heavy use: 5.6, 2.6, 12.8, 4.8

SOURCE: *2000 National Household Survey on Drug Abuse*, U.S. Department of Health and Human Services, Substance Abuse and Mental Health Services Administration, Office of Applied Studies, 2001. CURRENT USE=any use in the past month. BINGE USE=five or more drinks on the same occasion on at least one day within the past month. HEAVY USE=five or more drinks on the same occasion on each of five or more days in the past month. Note: All "heavy alcohol users" are also "binge alcohol users."

Figure 11

Alcohol use among students

SOURCE: 2001 *Monitoring the Future Study*, Institute for Social Research, University of Michigan. EVER USED=alcohol use, "more than a few sips," at least once in lifetime. EVER BEEN DRUNK=consuming five or more drinks in a row on a single occasion at least once. PAST YEAR=any use in the past year. CURRENT USE=any use in the past month.

and 20% were for alcohol with a secondary drug. For the alcohol-only clients, 5% were under age twenty, and 77% were age thirty and older. For the alcohol-with-secondary-drug admissions, 12% were under age twenty, and 64% were age thirty and older. The average age at admission to treatment was thirty-eight for alcohol only and thirty-three for alcohol with a secondary drug. About three-quarters of admissions were male.[18]

Recent Developments

Underage drinking remains a social problem of enormous proportion and complexity. The dangers related to alcohol use among youth extend beyond the tragedy of alcohol-related traffic fatalities, accidents, drownings, and suicides.

A recent research study by the National Institute on Alcohol Abuse and Alcoholism found that the younger someone starts drinking, the more likely that person is to develop alcohol dependence. The study, the largest of its kind worldwide, analyzed data from the National Longitudinal Alcohol Epidemiologic Survey that interviewed 27,616 people.[19]

Among respondents who began drinking before the age of fifteen, more than 40% were classified as alcohol dependent at some point in their lifetime. Yet among respondents who began drinking at the age of twenty-one and twenty-two, only 10% became alcohol dependent at some point in their lifetime. The same patterns held true for the development of alcohol abuse. These findings suggest that delaying the onset of drinking among young people may significantly reduce the risk of future alcohol-related problems.[20]

Widespread underage alcohol use occurs amid cultural norms that, to some extent, look the other way or see it as an acceptable rite of passage into adulthood. Children are exposed to alcohol advertising at very young ages, particularly catchy ads on TV during major league sporting events. They also observe alcohol use by their parents and families, which may or may not be accompanied by messages that help children understand the concept of appropriate use.

We tend not to tackle underage drinking head-on. Perhaps our heavy-handed emphasis on discouraging illegal drug abuse has inadvertently resulted in greater tolerance of alcohol use by young people as somehow the lesser of two evils.

Many of today's parents grew up when the legal drinking age was eighteen. Consequently, they tend to voice little, if any, objection to alcohol use among their eighteen-year-old children—as long as they don't drive. Too often, adults send the message that drinking among adolescents is acceptable as long as they don't get behind the wheel of a car, and the other dangers are deemphasized.

Another variation on the underage drinking problem

is binge drinking on college campuses. In recent years, several high-profile deaths due to alcohol poisoning have occurred as part of fraternity initiation ritual parties at prominent U.S. universities. A large body of research documents not only the widespread practice of binge drinking on college campuses but also higher rates of binge drinking among sorority and fraternity members than other students.[21] Various drinking games abound. These are group activities, and the goal is invariably to drink alcohol to intoxication.

In some circles, a person tries to drink twenty-one shots of alcohol from one minute after midnight on the date of their twenty-first birthday until the bar closes. In states where bars close at 1 A.M. this is known as the "power hour." When two people race to see who can consume a case of beer first, it is known as a "case race."

"My parents were having trouble. I didn't feel like anybody loved me. I tried to commit suicide. And after that, alcohol became the only love in my life."

— seventeen-year-old girl, a recovering addict

Young people often look for ways to get the effects of alcohol more quickly. One practice is to put a long, flexible plastic tube down a person's throat directly into the stomach. With a funnel attached to the exterior end of the tube, large amounts of alcoholic beverages are poured directly into the stomach—entire pitchers of beer, for example. This allows the ingestion of a large volume of alcohol in the briefest time possible. This practice, known as "beer bonging," occurs not only at private parties but also in public bars and restaurants. There are also isolated reports of people injecting alcohol intravenously to avoid the telltale smell of alcohol on their breath. It is important to understand that such practices can and do lead to acute alcohol toxicity and death.

8. Cocaine

Observable Indications of Use	Rapid speech/talkativeness High energy level/restlessness Dry mouth Dilated pupils Redness around nose Runny nose
Effects of Use	Increased mental alertness Increased physical energy Elevated mood/euphoria Loss of appetite Extreme weight loss with prolonged use Insomnia Paranoia Increased body temperature Increased heart rate Elevated blood pressure
Duration of Effects	15–30 minutes for powder cocaine (hydrochloride) snorted 5–10 minutes for crack (cocaine base) smoked
Signs of Overdose	Heart palpitations Body tremors Heart attack Stroke Seizures Respiratory arrest
Fatal Overdose Possible	Yes, from heart attack, respiratory arrest, or stroke **IMPORTANT: If you suspect a person may have overdosed on cocaine, call 911 and seek emergency medical treatment immediately.**

Cocaine is a central nervous system stimulant derived from the cocoa plant. In parts of South America, the leaves of the cocoa plant are chewed or brewed in tea for their stimulant effects and to prevent altitude sickness. Cocaine is also used medically in the United States as a topical anesthetic in nose and throat surgery.

Types of Cocaine

Cocaine hydrochloride, the white crystal powder, is also known as coke, blow, snow, C, flake, or nose candy. It is chopped into a fine powder, usually laid out in lines (narrow strips several inches long), and then snorted up the nose. It is also injected intravenously.[1]

Small, hard chunks of cocaine are **cocaine base,** also known as crack, ready rock, gravel, rock, or freebase. Crack is heated in a pipe, and its vapors are inhaled. Crack can also be dissolved and injected, but it's not as commonly injected as cocaine hydrochloride.[2]

Cocaine is also used in combination with other illicit drugs. Cocaine combined with heroin and injected is known as a speedball.

Effects and Consequences of Use

Cocaine illustrates how the route of administration can affect the addictive potential of a drug. Because the vapors from crack are absorbed through the lungs, the drug reaches the brain within seconds, delivering a strong surge known to the user as a rush. With injection, cocaine reaches the brain in about fifteen to thirty seconds, and with snorting, within three to five minutes.

The faster the absorption of the drug, the more intense the initial blast of euphoria. The more rewarding the rush, the greater the craving. The greater the craving, the more likely users are to develop chronic abuse patterns and addiction. For these reasons, some generally regard crack as more addictive than other types of cocaine, although crack's perceived addictiveness is primarily a function of how quickly cocaine reaches the brain by smoking versus snorting.[3]

Why do drug users develop cravings? Because the neurochemical circuits of the brain define the rush as rewarding, they send out chemical messages urging the user to repeat the experience as soon as possible. With crack, the effects can wear off within ten minutes, and with cocaine hydrochloride, within fifteen to thirty minutes.[4] After repeated use, the peak high is accompanied by an equal and opposite low, characterized by fatigue, irritability, and dysphoria (the opposite of euphoria).

"I love cocaine. I used it in my twenties and never had any problems with it. But now that I'm over fifty I'm afraid it will give me a heart attack."

— fifty-two-year-old former cocaine user

Nonetheless, the cravings to repeat the euphoria of the initial use persist. As with other stimulants, however, prolonged use of cocaine results in tolerance, which means the user has to take increasing amounts of the drug to receive the same desired effect. The user seeks out more frequent and larger doses not only to avert the discomfort of withdrawal (to avoid the crash) but also to try to achieve the same initial rush.[5]

> **"I'll never forget the first time I did crack.
> All I could think about was, 'Where can I
> get some more of this stuff?'"**
>
> — a thirty-five-year-old recovering crack addict

Cocaine abuse has numerous adverse medical and health effects. Cocaine use reduces blood flow to the heart, causes serious irregularities in cardiac rhythm, and can precipitate cardiac arrest. Cocaine also reduces blood flow to multiple regions of the brain. Recent research suggests that these repeated reductions in blood flow to the brain, along with elevated blood pressure, increase the likelihood of stroke. Reduced blood flow also slows thought processes, causes memory problems, and makes concentration difficult.[6] In addition, chronic reduced blood flow to the bowel can produce bowel gangrene and other abdominal problems.[7]

The combination of cocaine and alcohol poses a unique medical threat. Researchers have discovered that when cocaine and alcohol combine in the liver, a third substance, *cocaethylene,* is produced. It is more toxic and longer acting than either cocaine or alcohol alone and possibly increases the risk of sudden death. The National Institute on Drug Abuse notes that the combination of cocaine and alcohol is the most prevalent combination that results in drug-related death.[8]

Because the vapors of crack are very hot and the pipes very short, chronic users often develop serious lung problems, occasional chest pains, and open sores around the mouth and lips. Chronic snorters can lose the sense of smell and develop nosebleeds, septum deviation, a persistent runny nose, and nasal congestion.[9]

Primary User Groups

The peak of what has been called the cocaine epidemic occurred in the mid-1980s. Cocaine use has declined significantly since 1985, when an estimated 5.7 million people in the United States (3% of the population over age twelve) were current users.[10]

In 2000 an estimated 1.2 million people, or 0.5% of the U.S. population age twelve and older, reported current cocaine use. Cocaine use is most prevalent among people age eighteen to twenty-five, with 1.4% of that group reporting current use, compared with 0.8% of people age twenty-six to thirty-four.[11] The average age of first use is estimated at 19.5 years.[12]

Cocaine use among students in 2001 was reported by 1.2% of eighth graders, 1.3% of tenth graders, and 2.1% of high school seniors. Current cocaine use among high school seniors also peaked in 1985, just as it did for adults. In that year 6.7% of seniors reported using cocaine in the past month.[13]

Although a relatively small proportion of the population uses cocaine, its use results in more hospital emergency room episodes than any other illicit drug. This is due to the many acute medical complications produced by cocaine use. Cocaine was present in 29% of emergency department episodes in 2000 (174,881 mentions); almost a quarter of the episodes were attributed to crack cocaine. Cocaine mentions were stable from 1994 to 2000, with 71 per 100,000 population in 2000.[14]

Of all treatment admissions, 14.4% were for cocaine in 1999, most of which (73%) were for crack cocaine.[15] Only 2.2% were people under the age of twenty, and 76.6% were age thirty and older. The average age at admission was 34.9 years. Males accounted for 57% and females 43%. Cocaine treatment admissions declined 16% from 1995 to 1999.[16]

Recent Developments

In the 1980s crack cocaine took hold in the United States, in part because of the strong rush it delivered, but also because of its packaging. For the first time, a piece of crack cocaine could be purchased for only ten dollars. Before then most cocaine was powder that was sold for one hundred dollars a gram. Cocaine use overall declined substantially since the 1980s. Yet because cocaine is such a powerful and damaging drug, the medical consequences associated with cocaine abuse still outnumber those associated with any other illicit drug.

Older Users

While cocaine use is still most prevalent among people age eighteen to twenty-five, there have been some relatively recent shifts. The rate of new initiates into cocaine use among adolescents (age twelve through seventeen) and young adults (age eighteen through twenty-five) declined from the 1980s until the early 1990s. Data from the Arrestee Drug Abuse Monitoring (ADAM) program reveal that, in most cities, older arrestees are more likely to test positive for cocaine than younger arrestees. In 1997 in Washington, D.C., for example, 5% of youthful arrestees (age fifteen to twenty) tested positive for cocaine, compared with nearly half of older arrestees (age thirty-six and older).[17]

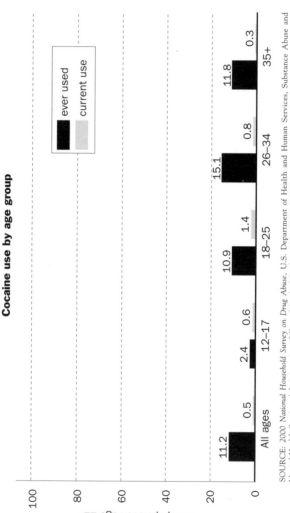

Figure 12

Cocaine use by age group

% of population age 12+

- ever used
- current use

Age group	ever used	current use
All ages	11.2	0.5
12–17	2.4	0.6
18–25	10.9	1.4
26–34	15.1	0.8
35+	11.8	0.3

SOURCE: 2000 *National Household Survey on Drug Abuse*, U.S. Department of Health and Human Services, Substance Abuse and Mental Health Services Administration, Office of Applied Studies, 2001. EVER USED=any use in lifetime. CURRENT USE=any use in past month.

Figure 13

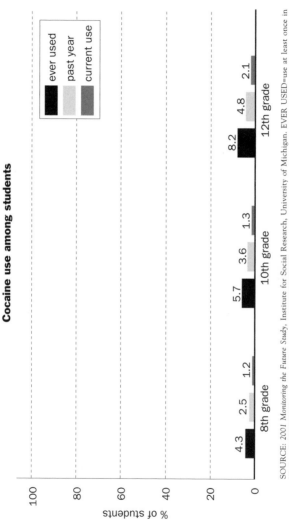

Cocaine use among students

SOURCE: *2001 Monitoring the Future Study*, Institute for Social Research, University of Michigan. EVER USED=use at least once in lifetime. PAST YEAR=any use in the past year. CURRENT USE=any use in the past month.

Figure 14

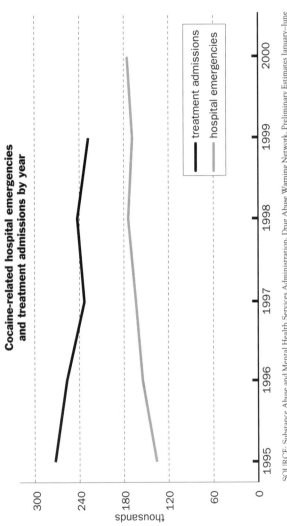

Cocaine-related hospital emergencies and treatment admissions by year

legend: — treatment admissions — hospital emergencies

thousands

300   240   180   120   60   0

1995   1996   1997   1998   1999   2000

SOURCE: Substance Abuse and Mental Health Services Administration, Drug Abuse Warning Network, Preliminary Estimates January–June 2001 with Revised Estimates 1994–2000, DHHS publication no. (SMA) 02-3634, and *Treatment Episode Data Set: 1994–1999*, DHHS publication no. (SMA) 01-3550.

Female Users

While cocaine use has declined overall, the drop in use is more apparent among males than females. Cocaine appears to have maintained a stronghold among women. In many cities, more female than male arrestees test positive for cocaine. This is attributed, in large part, to the phenomenon of trading sex for crack.[18]

"When you're all freaked out on coke, I mean, you got people bustin' each other over the head for five dollars. Irrational, paranoid behavior, you know, when they're all strung out on the stuff. And they got crack out on the street. . . . You can spend ten dollars and catch a buzz, but in the long run once you get started on that ten dollars, you're gonna go out and spend two hundred dollars. With cocaine you just don't know. They might be so paranoid one time, I mean, that they got a gun out shootin' at noises."

— an opiate addict, in reference to crack users

9. Hallucinogens

Observable Indications of Use	Bewildered appearance May appear out of touch with immediate environment Difficulty in speaking Garbled speech Disorientation Loss of coordination Easily agitated (with PCP) Dilated pupils
Effects of Use	Poor perception of time, movement, temperature, and distance Synesthesia (blending of senses) Hallucinations (at high doses) Possible nausea Visual distortions (at low doses) Perspiration or chills Body tremors Increased heart rate Elevated blood pressure Increased pulse
Duration of Effects	Variable, depending on the amount and substance
Signs of Overdose	Trancelike state Fearful or terrified state Psychotic episode PCP only: drooling, eyes flicking up and down, seizures, dizziness, drop in blood pressure and respiration
Fatal Overdose Possible	Yes, PCP only, from cardiac arrest, respiratory arrest, or stroke **IMPORTANT: If you suspect a person may have overdosed on PCP, call 911 and seek emergency medical treatment immediately.**

Hallucinogens comprise a broad category of natural and synthetic substances that, when ingested, dramatically alter the user's perception of reality. Because the *effects* of these substances are so similar, the information in the chart on page 117 applies to all hallucinogens discussed here.

This chapter also includes some anesthetic drugs, PCP and ketamine, that are not hallucinogens per se but are abused for their hallucinogenic effects. MDMA (Ecstasy), a methamphetamine also abused for its hallucinogenic properties, will be discussed briefly here and more extensively in chapter 13, "Methamphetamine/Stimulants" (see page 187).

Types of Hallucinogens

Peyote

The *peyote cactus* contains a psychoactive substance called mescaline that is found in small crowns (called buttons) located on the top of the plant. These buttons are soaked in water to obtain a hallucinogenic liquid or dried and then chewed. Peyote is known as peyote buttons, button, cactus, or mescaline. The first effect upon ingestion is usually nausea. Five grams of dried peyote create effects that last up to twelve hours. Mescaline can also be produced synthetically. Peyote is used in some Native American religious ceremonies.[1]

Psilocybin

Psilocybin mushrooms are native to Mexico and Central America and can also be cultivated indoors. They are known as shrooms or mush. They are eaten dried or fresh or combined with loose-leaf marijuana in a joint and smoked. About two grams of dried mushrooms produce effects that last up to six hours.[2] The effects are less pronounced than those from mescaline and LSD. In low doses, the effects are more akin to visual distortions of light and geometry than to full-blown, psychedelic hallucinations.

Other Hallucinogenic Plants

A type of sage plant, *Salvia divinorum*, also known as diviner's sage, can be smoked or chewed or brewed in tea. When ingested its effects include intense hallucinations, out-of-body experiences, sensations of time travel or merging with inanimate objects, short-term memory loss, and unconsciousness. Effects last for about an hour.

Jimsonweed, Datura stramonium, is an annual, flowering, noxious plant that grows wild in North America. It is also known as Jamestown weed, Angel's Trumpet, Devil's Trumpet, loco weed, or thorn apple. As a drug of abuse, it can be smoked, eaten, chewed, or brewed in tea. The small black seeds are the most toxic. Drug effects include powerful hallucinations, blurred vision, agitation, incoherent speech, hyperthermia, difficulty swallowing, dried mucous membranes, and combative behavior.

Because the digestive process is slowed, the effects can last for twenty-four to forty-eight hours, according to the National Drug Intelligence Center. It is not a controlled substance in the United States although at least three states—Connecticut, New Jersey, and Tennessee—have passed legislation in an attempt to control it. There is no antidote for jimsonweed poisoning, and deaths have occurred among teenagers taking it recreationally.

Morning glory seeds are sometimes ingested for hallucinogenic effects. Nausea typically precedes the onset of psychoactive effects, and use can produce convulsions.

LSD (Lysergic Acid Diethylamide)

LSD is the most potent synthetic hallucinogen. Commonly known as acid, it is sold in dosage units of small tablets (called microdots); tiny, clear, gelatin-like squares (known as windowpanes); or, most often, one-quarter-inch-square pieces of paper (known as blotter acid). All are taken orally.[3]

Blotter acid is made by spraying or dripping liquid LSD onto a sheet of absorbent blotter-type paper. The paper is then either sold in a full sheet of one hundred units or subdivided into individual dosage units. The blotter paper typically has different characters, logos, or geometric patterns printed on it before it is infused with LSD. Some sheets of LSD, for example, have Beavis and Butthead figures, flying Pegasus, Superman, the Golden

Arches, peace symbols, or even law enforcement logos.

The average dosage unit today is 20 to 80 micrograms, compared with 250 to 300 micrograms in the 1960s.[4] The lower dose of today's LSD may account for the relatively lower number of medical emergencies associated with the drug. The effects last up to twelve hours. LSD does produce tolerance but typically not the compulsive and frequent drug-seeking behavior that is characteristic of other drugs of abuse.[5]

Because LSD is so long-acting, a user who becomes uncomfortable with the effects is in for a long ride. Users experience strong changes in mood and report something like a short circuit of sensory perceptions. They might experience synesthesia, where they "hear" visual images or "see" noises. Adverse reactions can resemble psychotic, even catatonic, states. Users may withdraw to a pattern of repetitive motion, for example, or exhibit violent or unpredictable behavior.

A flashback is when a user later reexperiences the sensations of LSD intoxication, sometimes months after the effects of the drugs have dissipated. This phenomenon is also known as "hallucinogen persisting perception disorder" when it causes substantial psychological distress.[6] Some users report flashbacks that are not problematic. The use of LSD can also precipitate profound, long-lasting psychiatric conditions such as schizophrenia or depression, although the exact role of LSD in these instances is unknown.[7]

Phencyclidine (PCP)

PCP is an illicit anesthetic drug that produces hallu-cinogen-like effects and bizarre behavior. It's known as angel dust, hog, wack, water, dust, animal tranquilizer, or rocket fuel. Marijuana joints or blunts that contain PCP are called love boats, sherms, dust blunts, or happy sticks. A 1998 Texas study of dipped marijuana joints used by adolescents found that most joints allegedly treated with formaldehyde (known as fry, amp, or wets) actually contained a mixture of both formaldehyde and PCP.[8] PCP-dipped joints and cigarettes have a distinc-tive, pungent chemical smell. Crack that has been dipped in PCP is known as space dust.

PCP was used as an anesthetic first with humans and eventually only with animals. According to the U.S. Drug Enforcement Administration, nearly all PCP used illegally today is manufactured in clandestine labs. It is sold as a liquid, powder, tablet, gummy mass, or capsule that may be light tan or white. Other chemically related, illicitly manufactured substances that produce similar effects are PCE and TCP.[9]

As with other drugs, the duration of effects varies by dose, but they can last up to a few days. Neither toler-ance nor withdrawal has been observed. Indications of use include an unusual gait; fast, involuntary eye move-ments; and a distant demeanor. At low doses, pulse and respiration accelerate, and at higher doses they drop.

PCP in large doses produces a profoundly altered state. A user's sense of consciousness, identity, memory, and environment, which are usually interrelated, falls apart. Numbness or rigidity of extremities, large motor dysfunction, jerking eye movements, auditory hallucinations, nausea, drooling, dizziness, and memory loss have been reported.[10] The user feels detached from the physical environment and at times stares blankly, paralyzed to the point of being unable to move or speak.

"PCP made me realize what it must feel like to be profoundly retarded. Nothing about my body movements or speech worked the way it was supposed to. I felt like a moron and couldn't wait for the drug to wear off."

— onetime PCP user

Signs of overdose are seizures and coma. Death can occur from cardiac arrest, respiratory arrest, or stroke. PCP-related deaths often stem from accidental injuries because the users are so out of touch with the environment and lack motor control.[11]

What most distinguishes the use of PCP from other drugs in this category is the extreme manifestations of rage, power, strength, and invulnerability. PCP users can act out violently and appear impervious to physical pain, perhaps because of the drug's anesthetic properties. Some users have performed feats of incredible strength that they could not ordinarily accomplish. PCP can also produce severe psychotic reactions that resemble schizophrenia, paranoid delusions, and catatonia.[12] Chronic PCP users tend to exhibit marked memory and speech problems, even long after cessation of use.

Ketamine (Special K)

Ketamine, like PCP, is a depersonalizing, dissociative, anesthetic drug with hallucinogenic properties. It is also known as Special K, K, Ket, or Vitamin K. Being under the influence of ketamine is known as being in the hole, in K-land, or in the K-hole. The onset of effects varies by route of administration. Because the effects last one to two hours, ketamine is promoted as a shorter trip than LSD or PCP. It is typically sold at nightclubs and raves.[13]

Liquid ketamine is used legally in veterinary surgery to immobilize small animals such as cats. As a drug of abuse, it is diverted from veterinary sources, usually by burglary. It can be injected intramuscularly, but more often the liquid is changed into a powder, which is snorted, sprinkled on marijuana or tobacco and smoked, or mixed in beverages. It is sometimes pressed into tablets and taken orally.

The effects of ketamine resemble those from PCP and LSD, although they are less extreme. In low doses, it produces hallucinations, muscle rigidity, numbness, and impaired motor skills and speech. In larger doses, convulsions can occur, followed by loss of consciousness and a "flat-lined" or near death experience. Some users try to achieve an out-of-body state of suspended consciousness with ketamine. A pattern of daily use is not typical.

Ketamine is increasingly mixed with other drugs including methamphetamine (see page 190), MDMA (see below and page 191), cocaine (see page 105), and flunitrazepam (see page 209). G and K is a combination of GHB (see page 210) and ketamine. CK is cocaine and ketamine.[14]

MDMA (Ecstasy)

The compound 3,4-methylenedioxymethamphetamine, known as MDMA or Ecstasy, is a growing party drug of abuse among young people. It is a methamphetamine with hallucinogenic properties (see chapter 13, "Methamphetamine/Stimulants," for a complete description). However, it is used largely for its hallucinogenic effects by the same primary user groups that use hallucinogens such as LSD and PCP in party settings.

Effects and Consequences of Use

Generally speaking, the larger and stronger the dose, the more pronounced the hallucinogenic effects. In very low doses, the effects of hallucinogens are more stimulant-like, with only mild visual distortions. Perception of the physical and psychic world is altered, and the user may appear disconnected from the immediate environment.

Higher doses produce rich visual hallucinations that profoundly impair one's ability to interact normally with other people and situations. For this reason, people who are intoxicated on hallucinogens (known as tripping) behave in noticeably strange ways, as if something is "wrong" with them. Their perception of reality is markedly different from what a nonuser experiences, even though the two may be in the same setting at the same time.

At high doses, hallucinogen users are less able to shift their attention from the drug's effects or make the hallucinations stop or temporarily subside. This alone can produce anxiety. Bad trips occur when a user experiences negative anxiety or panic reactions while under the influence. People with preexisting mental disorders or emotional instability more often report these adverse reactions.

Some hallucinogens are naturally occurring substances. Others are produced synthetically. According to the U.S. Drug Enforcement Administration, several clandestine labs in northern California supply most of the country's LSD. Most MDMA is produced in Europe.[15]

Primary User Groups

Roughly 26.1 million Americans (11.7% of the population) have tried hallucinogens at least once in their lifetime, and 971,000 (0.4%) are current users.[16] Use is most prevalent among people age eighteen to twenty-five (1.8%) and least prevalent among those age thirty-five and older.[17]

Among students, the likelihood of trying hallucinogens increases with age. Among high school seniors, 12.8% have used at least once, as have 7.8% of tenth graders and 4% of eighth graders.[18]

In 2001, 3.2% of high school seniors, 2.1% of tenth graders, and 1.2% of eighth graders reported current hallucinogen use, mostly LSD.[19]

In recent years hospital emergencies for LSD have declined, while those for MDMA (Ecstasy), GHB, and PCP have increased significantly. (See figure 17.) From 1997 to 2000 hospital emergency room mentions of MDMA rose from 637 to 4,511; PCP rose from 3,626 to 5,404; and GHB rose from 762 to 4,969. When compared with other drugs of abuse, however, MDMA, ketamine, and GHB emergency room episodes are relatively infrequent, with 2 per 100,000 population in 2000.[20] Also consider that the rise in PCP episodes may be due, in large part, to the practice of combining PCP and PCP/formaldehyde mixtures with marijuana.

Relatively few people who seek addiction treatment report hallucinogens as the primary substance problem (0.2%); more than half of these people (56%) were under the age of twenty. Males accounted for 75%.[21]

Figure 15

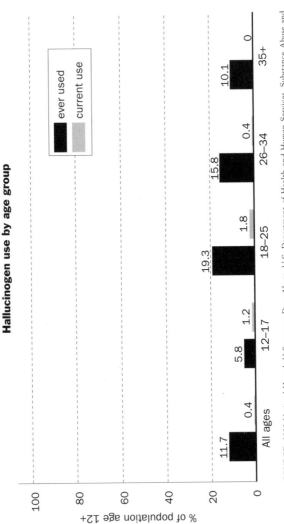

Hallucinogen use by age group

% of population age 12+

Age group	ever used	current use
All ages	11.7	0.4
12–17	5.8	1.2
18–25	19.3	1.8
26–34	15.8	0.4
35+	10.1	0

SOURCE: 2000 *National Household Survey on Drug Abuse*, U.S. Department of Health and Human Services, Substance Abuse and Mental Health Services Administration, Office of Applied Studies, 2001. EVER USED=any use in lifetime. CURRENT USE=any use in the past month.

Figure 16

Hallucinogen use among students

- ever used
- past year
- current use

% of students

8th grade: 4.0, 2.5, 1.2

10th grade: 7.8, 5.2, 2.1

12th grade: 12.8, 8.4, 3.2

SOURCE: *2001 Monitoring the Future Study*, Institute for Social Research, University of Michigan. EVER USED=use at least once in lifetime. PAST YEAR=any use in the past year. CURRENT USE=any use in the past month.

Figure 17

Hospital emergencies for hallucinogens and club drugs by year

LSD hospital emergencies
PCP hospital emergencies
MDMA hospital emergencies
Ketamine hospital emergencies
GHB hospital emergencies

thousands

1995   1996   1997   1998   1999   2000

SOURCE: Substance Abuse and Mental Health Services Administration, Drug Abuse Warning Network. Preliminary Estimates January–June 2001 with Revised Estimates 1994–2000, DHHS publication no. (SMA) 02-3634, and *Treatment Episode Data Set: 1994–1999*, DHHS publication no. (SMA) 01-3550.

Recent Developments

Hallucinogens are historically among the most popular drugs of abuse by young people. Raves and late-night dance parties that cater to drug-using attendees continue, as do urban legends about LSD being sold to children. Internet sales of "research drugs" and on-line advice about how to use hallucinogens abound.

Raves

Raves are large events or parties with music, lights, dancing, and drugs.[22] Interested people hear about an upcoming rave by word of mouth, through advertising, or on the Internet. Colorful, hip promotional flyers announce the rave, the promoter, and the disc jockey. Titles of raves include "Euphoria," "Blurred Senseless," "Prepare Yourself," "Blackout," "Dream Ecstasy," and "Control." Raves can be found in big cities, suburbs, small towns, and rural areas.

Raves usually take place in warehouses or large buildings such as convention centers, sports arenas, or meeting halls but also happen outdoors in fields or other large, open areas. Raves feature DJs blasting techno-music, giant walls of sound, and cyber light shows ("visuals"). Many raves have "chill-out rooms" where partiers can go to take a break or chill out from the exhausting, high-energy night of dancing by taking a shower or being in air-conditioning.

Part of the mystique of a rave is that attendees don't always know its location until the last minute. People purchase a rave ticket at a retail store and return on the day of the event to get additional information announcing the exact location. Sometimes, when the rave is at a large convention center or sports arena, the location is known from the beginning.

Raves typically start around 10 or 11 P.M. Some last all night, and others break up at 2 or 4 A.M. Some raves don't admit people under the age of eighteen after midnight. Ticket prices range from ten to twenty-five dollars. Usually no alcohol is offered, but rather "smart drinks" are served—gimmicky beverages with natural additives that supposedly boost mental powers. Some raves are advertised for age twenty-one and over and have cash bars and stage shows.

Raves are primarily targeted at teenagers. They often get their parents' permission to attend by assuring them that no alcohol will be served, that it's just a dance party. But while it may be true that no alcohol is served at some raves, they are notorious for drug use.

Hallucinogenic drugs, especially Ecstasy, LSD, and mushrooms, are sold at raves by others in attendance. Rave attendees who are under the influence of MDMA are said to be "rolling." They also may wear disposable surgical masks that have been rubbed in over-the-counter mentholated cold products. This allegedly enhances the effects of MDMA. To avoid teeth grinding due to the effects of MDMA, some users also use pacifiers.[23] Alcohol allegedly reduces the effects of MDMA according to "ravers."

Some rave attendees buy many pills at the beginning of the evening and take them intermittently throughout the night, simultaneously use MDMA with other drugs, or unknowingly ingest pills sold as Ecstasy that do not actually contain MDMA. (See page 204 in chapter 13, "Methamphetamine/Stimulants," for information about MDMA combos.)

Most of the flyers promoting raves have hidden or overt references to the drug Ecstasy, such as a lowercase letter *e*, or an uppercase letter X, or a statement such as "Vitamin E not included." Balloons filled with either helium or nitrous oxide are also sold at raves for inhalation.

After the rave, attendees can hop on the Internet and either chat with other people who are just getting home or post their impressions of the rave where others can read them.

Club Drugs

Club drugs is a phrase used in reference to a group of drugs most likely to be found, sold, and used at nightclubs and raves. Some are uppers. Some are downers.

The actual menu of drugs found at clubs varies city to city and club to club. Sometimes this term includes all the hallucinogenic drugs mentioned in this chapter, plus heroin (see page 141), GHB (see page 210), and Rohypnol (see page 209). The National Institute on Drug Abuse currently uses the phrase *club drugs* in reference to LSD, MDMA, GHB, ketamine, Rohypnol, and methamphetamine.[24]

The problem with grouping drugs according to where they are used and sold is that it overlooks other drugs that are also present. In the case of nightclubs, other drugs typically present include alcohol, marijuana, cocaine, and sometimes heroin.

"When I took mushrooms, I was terrified and so scared! It was like I was being pulled away and was convinced I'd never be able to come back."

— onetime mushroom user

Club drugs come in many forms. GHB and GBL (gamma butyrolactones) are liquids. Rohypnol is a pill that is crushed and dissolved in beverages. Others are capsules, such as ketamine and MDMA, or small pieces of paper placed under the tongue, such as LSD.

Sometimes powdered hallucinogenic drugs are sold in capsules that contain a combination of substances. The person selling the capsules may use the combination angle as a marketing approach and a way to entice new users. The seller might say, for example, "This capsule has some MDMA to get you up, some meth to keep you up, and a touch of heroin to 'take the edge off.'" A little bit of this and a little bit of that. This packaging and marketing approach conveys a level of precision in dosing and effect that simply doesn't exist. To a young, inexperienced user, however, the capsule can make a potential drug experience look like a predictable, controllable proposition.

Armchair, On-line Pharmacologists

Visit any number of Web sites and you'll find a growing number of "armchair, on-line pharmacologists." These are typically experienced, chronic drug abusers who give out advice to other drug abusers, aspiring novice drug abusers, and would-be drug abusers on a number of topics: the correct dose of a drug, the anticipated effects, the duration of effects, the interaction of effects across various illicit and licit drugs, the suggested sequencing and timing of ingesting multiple drugs, the chemical makeup of a drug or specific tips on its manufacture or synthesis. Like the person promoting or selling Ecstasy at raves, they portray drug abuse as a benign, predictable, and controllable proposition, when in fact quite the opposite is true. These on-line drug aficionados often focus on the "proper" use of various hallucinogens, used alone and in combination with one another.

Internet Sales and "Research Drugs"

In addition to instant advice on the use and manufacture of various hallucinogens, it is also possible to directly purchase hallucinogens and other "club drugs" over the Internet. On-line sales of DMT, AMT, and DPT, all molecular variants of tryptamine (a naturally occurring compound found in the brain chemical serotonin), have been reported. Among these, AMT (alpha-methyltryptamine) is the fastest growing one of abuse. It is a white powder taken orally, taken intranassally, or smoked. Effects are similar to those of MDMA. It is also known as Amtrak or Amthrax.

Other substances, such as 2C-T-7 (also known as T-7, 7-Up, or Tripstasy), are sold as experimental research compounds, sometimes with warnings or disclaimers that they are not intended for human consumption. All of these chemicals are known to produce strong hallucinogenic effects and compose what has been called "the designer-drug underground."[25] Designer drugs are those which are close in chemical structure to state or federally controlled substances, but are not themselves illegal.

Sale of GHB and GHB analogs (related compounds) via the Internet also continues. See discussion on page 215.

The Urban Legend—LSD Tattoos

Since the 1980s a flyer containing false information about LSD "tattoos" has circulated throughout the

United States, reaching small rural towns and big cities alike.[26] The alarming flyer has appeared in almost every state. Well-intentioned but uninformed people who believe it to be true perpetuate it. It is known as the "Blue Star LSD Hoax."

This piece of modern folklore has key elements that have not changed in its twenty-year history. It begins: "A form of tattoo called 'Blue Star' is being sold to schoolchildren." According to the flyer, the tattoos can get a person high "just by touching them" and come on brightly colored paper with designs of cartoon characters that appeal to children (blue stars, Mickey Mouse, Bart Simpson, clowns). The flyer states that the tattoos have been laced with strychnine and that "young lives have been lost."

This alarmist one-page flyer always ends with a plea to reproduce the warning and to "distribute this within your community and workplace" in order to warn others before more lives are lost. It always ends with, "This is very serious—young lives have already been taken! This is growing faster than we can warn parents and professionals!" The alleged source of the information varies somewhat but is always a quasi-legitimate-appearing, although fictitious, institution such as a hospital or law enforcement agency.

The flyer has been circulated by electronic mail and reproduced and distributed by VFW posts, churches, day-care centers, health clinics, schools, government agencies, newspapers, hospitals, large national corporations, post offices, and private businesses. It is alarming but simply *not true*.

The LSD tattoo scare is a hoax.[27] There is no factual basis to these reports. There are no such things as LSD tattoos. No lives have been lost. Yet this false information frightens people into action, and that's how the hoax is perpetuated. This is an urban legend that continues to find prolonged life in unsuspecting, concerned, and largely well-meaning audiences who take it at face value and spread the alarm. This hoax is currently being studied in some college sociology and anthropology courses.[28]

The Blue Star LSD Hoax is a classic example of un-informed drug hysteria. Sometimes a government official eventually debunks the hoax, yet even when this does occur, the hoax somehow arises again and again, always finding new audiences willing to believe the worst.

If you see the Blue Star LSD flyer, remember: Do not be alarmed. This is a hoax. *Do not pass it on.*

PCP with Marijuana

Marijuana cigarettes are increasingly "dipped" into PCP or a combination of PCP and formaldehyde. The recent rise in PCP hospital emergencies is believed to be, in part, a reflection of this trend. Slang terms for the dipped joints vary, but include wets, wet sticks, happy sticks, sherms, love boats, fry, and amp. The immediate effects are unlike those of marijuana alone—more stimulant-like. And in the long term the damage can be similar to that from solvent abuse.

10. Heroin/Opiates/Narcotics

Observable Indications of Use	Droopy eyelids Sluggish, drowsy mannerisms Slowed speech Nodding off—periodically slipping into momentary lapses of sleep Constricted, "pinpoint" pupils that are not responsive to light Eyes show little or no responsiveness to light Possible track marks or infections at injection sites
Effects of Use	Euphoria Pain relief Slowed breathing Slowed pulse rate Nausea Lowered blood pressure Lowered body temperature
Duration of Effects	Heroin: 4–6 hours Methadone: up to 24 hours Prescription analgesics: variable
Signs of Overdose	Clammy skin Slow, shallow breathing Seizures Coma
Fatal Overdose Possible	Yes, due to respiratory arrest **IMPORTANT: If you suspect a person may have overdosed on heroin, opiates, or narcotics, call 911 and seek emergency medical treatment immediately.**

Opiate is a general term for drugs derived from the opium poppy. *Narcotic* refers to those poppy-derived drugs as well as similar synthetic medications used for pain relief. *Heroin* is the most widely abused illicit narcotic in the United States and, thus, the primary focus of this chapter.

Types of Heroin/Opiates/Narcotics

Prescription narcotics used medically for pain relief include codeine (Tylenol with codeine), hydrocodone (Vicodin), hydromorphone (Dilaudid), oxycodone (OxyContin, Percodan, Percocet), pentazocine (Talwin), propoxyphene (Darvon), meperidine (Demerol), and morphine (MS-Contin). Prescription narcotics are administered orally, injected, or taken as suppositories.

Methadone is used in the treatment of narcotic addiction. For many years methadone, itself a narcotic, has been used as a prescription medication in the treatment of heroin addiction. It blocks the euphoric effects of heroin without itself producing a comparable "high," reduces craving, and suppresses withdrawal for more than twenty-four hours. It is typically used in outpatient settings. Some patients receive it indefinitely (known as methadone maintenance), while others eventually choose abstinence. Methadone is sometimes diverted from its legitimate use, sold on the illegal market, and used as a drug of abuse. Less than 20% of heroin addicts in the United States are treated with methadone, according to the National Institute on Drug Abuse.[1] LAAM (levo-alpha-acetyl-methadol) is another, longer-acting (up to seventy-two hours) synthetic opiate used in the treatment of heroin addiction.

Opium, made from the opium poppy, contains morphine and codeine and is medically prescribed in the treatment of acute diarrhea. It is also used medicinally in other cultures as a remedy for a variety of ailments and is eaten or smoked.

Narcotic addicts, when faced with shortages in their supply, often substitute various narcotic drugs for one another.

Heroin, which is not approved for medical use in the United States, is the most commonly abused street narcotic. Derived from the opium poppy, heroin is a white, brown, or tan powder. Black tar heroin is the exception; it appears as black, glasslike chunks or tarry balls because of its different processing method. Heroin is also known as junk, horse, H, gunpowder, smack, bomb, chiva, mud, noise, dope, or skag. Injecting heroin intravenously is known as mainlining or shooting up. The injection equipment is known as works, a fit, or a rig. Being under the influence of heroin is often referred to as being "on the nod."

Heroin can be injected intravenously, intramuscularly,

or subcutaneously (beneath the skin, known as skin popping). It may also be snorted or smoked. A relatively new route of heroin administration involves squirting or dripping heroin that has been dissolved in water up the nose from a small plastic bottle, a process known in Texas as shebanging.[2] Smoking heroin is known as chasing the dragon. Powdered heroin is laid in a line on a piece of tinfoil, which is heated from beneath; the vapors are then inhaled.

Intravenous injection of heroin produces an intense euphoric rush in less than ten seconds. Intramuscular injection produces a rush within five to eight minutes, and the effects of sniffing can be felt within ten to fifteen minutes.[3]

Heroin is sometimes used in combination with other illicit drugs. The most common combination is known as a speedball, which is heroin combined with cocaine.

Effects and Consequences of Use

Many narcotics abusers are polydrug abusers who have used other drugs of abuse in addition to narcotics. Some drug abusers use narcotics to lessen the withdrawal symptoms of other drugs of abuse, such as cocaine. Still others develop an addiction to prescribed narcotic pain medication, although this is quite rare.

At times, narcotic addicts may "doctor shop" to maintain a supply of prescribed narcotics. *Doctor shopping* refers

Chunks of crack cocaine (*far left*), a cocaine spoon filled with cocaine (cocaine hydrochloride powder) (*middle left*), and cocaine (*middle right*). A tightly rolled up piece of paper currency is often used as a straw to snort cocaine and other drugs intranasally.

Various types of pipes that are used to smoke crack cocaine

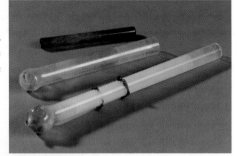

A vial used to carry cocaine with a small spoon attached to the lid (*far left*), a device designed to measure and dispense a single "hit" (dosage unit) of cocaine (*middle left*), a small vial containing a chunk of crack cocaine (*middle right*), and a small bottle that is used to carry or store cocaine or crack cocaine (*far right*)

Different types of LSD, known as blotter acid, are sold in sheets or by the individual dosage unit. Individual "hits" (dosage units) are wrapped in small pieces of aluminum foil.

A sheet that contains very small multiple doses of windowpane acid, a form of LSD

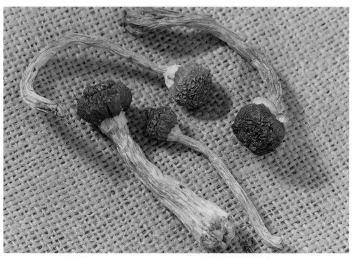

Four dried psilocybin mushrooms

Two different types of white heroin powder, a chunk of black tar heroin, and a syringe used for intravenous injection

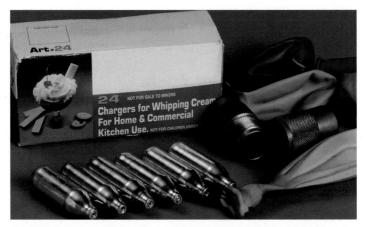

Small silver, sometimes lavender, canisters that contain nitrous oxide gas, known as "whippets," are sold as the propellant for making whipped cream. The two-piece screwable brass device releases the gas from the small canisters either directly into a person's mouth or nose or into a balloon.

Marijuana tops, known as "buds," lie beneath a hand-rolled marijuana cigarette, known as a "joint."

A marijuana cigarette, known as a "joint," shown with two packages of cigarette rolling papers, is surrounded by marijuana buds.

A variety of "roach clips" are used to hold a marijuana cigarette so it can be smoked in its entirety without burning the fingers or lips.

This collection of marijuana pipes includes a standard "one hitter" (*front left*), a small brass pipe that holds enough for one "hit" (dosage unit) and is stored in a wooden carrying case that also has a compartment for carrying marijuana (this device is also known as a "bat and dugout"). The large glass pipe (*center back*) is known as a "bong."

A piece of hashish, shown with a coin

Five tablets of MDMA, known as "Ecstasy," rest on a background of burlap. Note the different pastel colors, the different patterns imprinted on the top of the pills, and the variability in the width and height of each pill.

Two samples of methamphetamine, known as "crystal meth," are shown with a rolled-up dollar bill. The color variation is due to differences in the way it was made, the processing time, and the ingredients used.

Khat plants are shown wrapped in fresh banana leaves to preserve freshness. The khat leaves and stems are most often chewed but can also be brewed in tea.

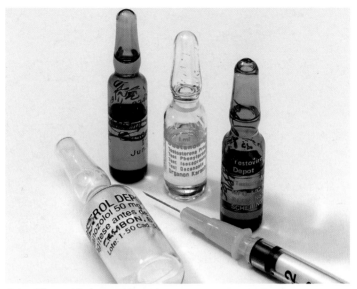

Injectable steroids shown with a syringe

These products contain either GHB or its chemical cousins GBL or 1,4-BD. Some labels describe the contents as a "dietary supplement" and others as an "organic cleaning solvent." Some bottles are unmarked.

to seeking out numerous doctors to treat concocted symptoms with prescribed narcotic drugs. In times of short supply, addicts may also purchase prescription narcotics that have been diverted into the black market.[4]

Chippers are people who only occasionally use heroin and are not physically dependent. In contrast, heroin addicts may inject four or more times daily. The course of heroin addiction can extend for decades with intermittent periods of abstinence.

> **"If I had never experienced [heroin], it wouldn't be there to haunt me."**
>
> — a heroin addict

The effects of heroin last from four to six hours, varying according to purity level and the tolerance of the user. Heroin purity varies considerably. Because too much pure heroin can result in respiratory arrest and death (overdose), an added danger of heroin use lies in the unpredictability of purity level. Street heroin has unknown purity, and when pharmaceutical narcotics of unknown strength are used, the results can be equally dangerous. Fentanyl, for example, is a prescription analgesic that is many times more potent than heroin. So even for experienced addicts, heroin overdose is a daily possibility, whether with street or pharmaceutical opiates. *China White* is a slang term for very high-purity heroin; when a substance is sold as China

White, it is purporting to be the best heroin around. Experienced heroin users generally reduce the dose accordingly, but inexperienced users can suffer serious consequences by failing to do so.

Because inert substances (cut) are mixed in with street heroin, there's a chance that some of the adulterants will not readily dissolve in the injectable solution and thereby block or clog blood vessels leading to various organs and parts of the body. This can cause bacterial infections of major organs (heart valves and lining, liver, kidney), blood vessels, or veins. Abscesses and other tissue infections may also occur at the injection sites. As mentioned earlier, injection drug use also carries the increased risk of acquiring and transmitting blood-borne pathogens like HIV, hepatitis, and other blood-borne diseases. Chronic injection drug abuse also contributes to collapsed veins.[5]

Regular heroin users develop a physical tolerance for it, requiring larger amounts of the drug to achieve the same effect. At that point, they use heroin and other narcotics both to avoid the pain of withdrawal (known as "getting sick") and to seek the effects (known as "getting well"). Heroin withdrawal occurs in addicts within hours

---

"Mainlined in the 1980s, heroin became mainstreamed in the 1990s."

of the last dose. Withdrawal ranges from mild flu-like symptoms to more severe reactions that can include an aching in the bones and muscles, cold flashes, vomiting, diarrhea, and agitation. Withdrawal symptoms peak at forty-eight to seventy-two hours and disappear within a week. The term *cold turkey* refers to sudden, complete withdrawal.

For addicts whose health is already compromised, sudden withdrawal from narcotics can be fatal. Pregnant mothers in methadone maintenance programs, for example, are not withdrawn from methadone before the baby's birth because of the increased risk of spontaneous abortion and premature birth. Some newborns are born dependent on methadone and withdraw under medical supervision after birth.

Most heroin entering the United States now originates in South America (65% of heroin seized in 1998) or Mexico (29%), not Southeast Asia. Today's heroin is of much higher purity than in the past, according to the U.S. Drug Enforcement Administration. In the 1980s purity levels ranged from 1% to 10%. The average estimated national purity level in 1980 was 3.6%. But by 1990 the average purity was estimated at 18%, and by 1998 at 41%. The price per dosage unit of pure heroin also dropped considerably.[6]

A significant consequence of the influx of very high-purity heroin was a change in the usual route of administration from injection to snorting and smoking. Heroin users no longer had to inject heroin to feel the effect. The purity was so high that the effects could be felt simply by snorting the drug (see "Heroin Snorting," page 149).

Primary User Groups

Heroin use among the general population is difficult to measure with precision. Few addicts live in traditional households with long-standing residency, and few are forthcoming about their use. Surveys grossly under-estimate this hidden population. That said, the estimated number of current heroin users in the United States ranges from 130,000 to 900,000. An estimated 2.8 million people have tried it at least once, and there are 130,000 current users, according to the 2000 National Household Survey on drug abuse.[7] About 104,000 people tried heroin for the first time in 1999. The average age of first use for new heroin initiates was 19.8 in 1999.[8]

Among students heroin use is low relative to other drugs of abuse, but it gradually increased in the middle to late 1990s. In 2001, current use was reported by less than 1% of students. Among high school seniors, 0.6% reported current use; among tenth graders, 0.3%; and among eighth graders, 0.4%.[9]

Hospital emergencies for heroin increased 36% from 1995 to 2000, with a 15% increase from 1999 to 2000 alone. The 94,804 emergency department mentions of heroin represent a rate of 38 per 100,000 population (compared with 71 per 100,000 for cocaine and 39 for marijuana).[10]

In 1999 more admissions to treatment were for opiates (mostly heroin) than for any other illicit drug, accounting for 16.2% of all treatment admissions. Only 3% of the heroin-related admissions to addiction treatment programs were people under the age of twenty. Seventy-two percent were age thirty and older. Males accounted for 67% and females 33%.[11]

The recent decline in heroin injection and increase in snorting is clearly reflected in national treatment data. Injection declined from 77% of heroin treatment admissions in 1992 to 66% in 1999.[12]

Recent Developments

The nature of heroin abuse has changed over the past decade.[13] There are new suppliers of the drug, new methods of use, and younger users.

Heroin Snorting

The recent influx of low-cost, high-purity South American heroin, coupled with a growing awareness of the dangers of HIV and hepatitis transmission from injection drug use, prompted a change in the usual route of heroin

Figure 18

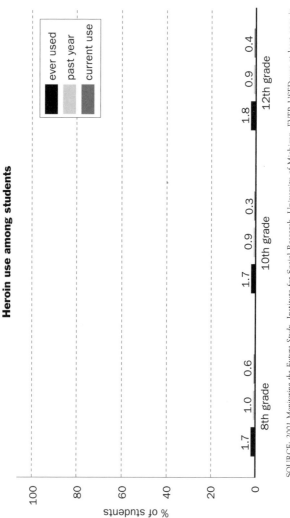

Heroin use among students

SOURCE: 2001 *Monitoring the Future Study*, Institute for Social Research, University of Michigan. EVER USED=use at least once in lifetime. PAST YEAR=any use in the past year. CURRENT USE=any use in the past month.

Figure 19

Heroin-related hospital emergencies and treatment admissions by year

treatment admissions

hospital emergencies

300
240
180
120
60
0

thousands

1995 1996 1997 1998 1999 2000

SOURCE: Substance Abuse and Mental Health Services Administration, Drug Abuse Warning Network, Preliminary Estimates January–June 2001 with Revised Estimates 1994–2000, DHHS publication no. (SMA) 02-3634, and *Treatment Episode Data Set: 1994–1999*, DHHS publication no. (SMA) 01-3550.

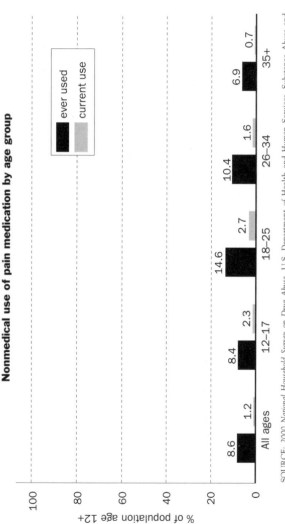

Figure 20

Nonmedical use of pain medication by age group

SOURCE: *2000 National Household Survey on Drug Abuse*, U.S. Department of Health and Human Services, Substance Abuse and Mental Health Services Administration, Office of Applied Studies, 2001. EVER USED=any use in lifetime. CURRENT USE=any use in past month.

administration from injection to snorting. Fewer users inject heroin; more snort or smoke it.

With the shift away from injection, heroin use seems more attractive. Gone are the powerful psychological and mechanical barriers of having to inject the drug. For many individuals, the idea of injecting anything, no matter how pleasurable the effect, is simply frightening, distasteful, and too much to overcome.

But with the new high-purity heroin, people can suddenly try it simply by snorting, the same way they use cocaine. They don't need to use a syringe or learn how to inject at all. Snorting and smoking leave no telltale syringe or other paraphernalia, no injection scars, no mess, no fear, and minimal bother.

Without syringe use, the fear of HIV transmission and AIDS diminished. Also gone are the fear and stigma of becoming a strung-out junkie with a needle in the arm. Many rookie heroin snorters even believe (falsely) that as long as they just snort the drug, there is no danger of becoming addicted.[14]

The New Heroin Users

In the final decade of the twentieth century, changes in the way heroin was used prompted the birth of a new, younger group of heroin users. For the first time, heroin started showing up in high schools, at rave parties, and in nightclubs. Heroin was blithely tooted up noses at private parties and fraternities, or in the privacy of back rooms and parked cars, just as cocaine had been twenty years earlier.

Heroin was even crushed and put into capsules for those who wanted exotic mixed combinations. The capsules sometimes contained other drugs, such as MDMA (Ecstasy) or cocaine; heroin was just part of the mix. It was not just for junkies anymore; heroin joined the nightclub crowd, no longer banished by the bloody syringe. Mainlined in the 1980s, heroin became mainstreamed in the 1990s.

> **"It's the best feeling in the world. It [heroin] totally envelopes you. It was like having a sexual orgasm times fifty to one hundred."**
>
> — a fifty-year-old recovering heroin addict, twenty-five years clean

In 1993, for the first time, more heroin snorters than injectors entered treatment programs in New York City. Among high school seniors in Miami, heroin use rose from 0.9% in 1993 to 2% in 1997 (four times the national rate at the time). In Denver, college parties suddenly had heroin as the new nose candy on the menu.[15] In Plano, Texas, an affluent suburb of Dallas, heroin overdoses killed nineteen young people between 1996 and 1998.[16] For ten dollars, Plano high school students bought capsules of Mexican chiva (heroin) with purity levels that ranged up to 75%. In suburban Chicago, young women influenced by the heroin-chic of fashion and music quietly became heroin users.

To the youthful drug abusers coming of age in the sixties, seventies, and eighties, heroin was the ultimate hard drug. It was the one they didn't mess around with. It was what separated them from those "other" people with "serious" drug habits. Shooting up? Too dangerous; too hard-core. Shooting up became a line drawn in the sand that most abusers didn't cross. In the 1990s and into the new century, that line has been washed away by a wave of high-purity, low-cost heroin. Heroin's just another drug at the party buffet.

The effects of this phenomenon have yet to be fully realized. Indications of a growing heroin problem among younger users are apparent in many cities.

But what if heroin purity declines, as is often the case once a "new" drug takes hold and establishes a loyal following? There's concern that the snorters, ever chasing after the same initial blast, will turn to heroin injection after all, despite the attendant risks and consequences. [17]

Prescription Drug Abuse and the Special Case of OxyContin

Used as medically directed, prescription medications can improve functioning and change lives. In 1999, however, an estimated four million Americans over age twelve used prescription medications for nonmedical purposes: pain medications (2.6 million); sedatives and tranquilizers (1.3 million); and stimulants (0.9 million).[18] Roughly 1.6 million used prescription pain relievers non-medically for the first time that year—four times as many as in 1980. The largest increase in new, nonmedical use of prescription drugs occurred in people age twelve to seventeen and those eighteen to twenty-five. See figure 20. From 1990 to 1998, the number of first-time non-medical users of prescription pain relievers rose 181%, stimulants rose 165%, tranquilizers rose 132%, and sedatives rose 90%.[19]

Oxycodone, a semi-synthetic, opioid analgesic medically prescribed for mild to moderate pain control, chronic pain syndromes, and treatment of terminal cancer pain, was produced in a continuous release form in 1996. OxyContin has an eight- to twelve-hour duration of action. OxyContin abuse, fatal overdoses, and black market sales of OxyContin have increased significantly in recent years.[20]

OxyContin is diverted by way of pharmacy theft, "doctor shopping," and improper prescribing by unscrupulous physicians. OxyContin is sought out and abused by seasoned drug abusers for its strong, heroin-like, euphoric effects. The pills are crushed and then either snorted or cooked down and injected to overcome the time-release mechanism. Many drug abusers prefer the predictable purity level that comes with a prescribed drug versus one purchased on the street, such as heroin.

Entrepreneurs hoping to cash in on its resale value in the illicit market, in particular drug abusers and dealers and those living on extremely limited incomes, also seek out OxyContin. A bottle of one hundred 40 mg tablets that sells at a retail pharmacy for $400 can have a resale value of $2,000 to $4,000 in the illicit market. Hence, even some people who have legitimate prescriptions find themselves unable to resist the lure of significantly boosting their incomes by the resale of their OxyContin.

"I'm gonna crave opiates as long as I live. That's deep."

— a heroin addict

11. Inhalants/Solvents

Observable Indications of Use	A conspicuous, strong chemical odor Paint stains on face, body, or clothing Finding a stash of chemical products in unusual locations, like a child's bedroom Purchasing increased amounts of household chemical products Drunk, dazed, dizzy demeanor Staggered gait Slurred speech Excitability followed by drowsiness Red or runny eyes or nose Rash or sores around the mouth
Effects of Use	Blurred vision Euphoria with hallucinations Reduced muscle coordination Nausea Intense headache Oxygen deprivation Irregular heartbeat Increased heart rate
Duration of Effects	5–60 minutes after sniffing ceases
Signs of Overdose	Loss of consciousness Respiratory arrest Cardiac arrest Coma
Fatal Overdose Possible	Yes, from Sudden Sniffing Death Syndrome or suffocation **IMPORTANT: If you suspect a person may have overdosed on inhalants or solvents, call 911 and seek emergency medical treatment immediately.**

Inhalants and *solvents* generally refer to a variety of chemical products, the vapors of which are intentionally inhaled to produce mood-altering effects. Hundreds of common household and industrial products, none of which were ever intended for human consumption, can be purposefully used to alter perception and mood.

Fumes are inhaled through the nose or mouth. Sometimes the products are put on wet rags and then placed near the mouth and nose or sprayed into small bags and inhaled from there. Some pressurized gases, such as nitrous oxide, are available in small pressurized containers that are sold and used as whipped cream propellant. The gas is released from the container into a balloon and then inhaled. Inhaling these chemical fumes through the mouth is called huffing. People who abuse inhalants are known as sniffers or huffers.[1]

Types of Inhalants/Solvents

There are three major types of products:

1. **Solvents:** gasoline, kerosene, glues, cements, nail polish remover, lighter fluid, paint thinners, degreasers, dry cleaning fluid, markers, correction fluid

2. **Gases/propellants:** propellants used in butane lighters; any aerosols, such as spray paints, hair spray, fabric protector, refrigerants; and medical anesthetic gases, such as nitrous oxide (used as a propellant in whipped cream), ether, or chloroform

3. **Volatile nitrites:** amyl nitrite, a cloth-covered vial that is snapped in half to release the vapor (once legitimately used by people with heart conditions and since replaced by nitroglycerin); and butyl and isobutyl nitrite, both sold over-the-counter as room deodorizers

Effects and Consequences of Use

Because inhalant and solvent abuse involves substances that were never intended for human consumption, the effects are extremely variable. There is no safe recommended dose. These toxic substances dissolve varnish, oil, and paint. The containers warn us to use them only in well-ventilated areas. These petrochemicals fuel engines and degrease, bond, or lubricate metal parts. They waterproof, clean, polish, or remove stains from fabric, carpets, furniture, and floors. They kill bugs, weeds, and other living organisms. The damage such products can inflict on human body tissue and organs is substantial.

The chemicals travel through the lungs and to the brain in high concentrations within seconds of inhalation. The initial rush from inhalants lasts at least several minutes and up to an hour. A user may feel light-headed or dizzy and experience true hallucinations (not just visual distortions). Other short-term effects of inhalants include feelings of euphoria and excitability followed by drowsiness.[2]

The major lasting damage from inhalant abuse occurs in the body's nervous system. Inhalants can destroy the protective fatty layer around the nerves themselves, which results in dementia and brain dysfunction. This may show up as a change in personality, the inability to think analytically, loss of memory, anxiety, hostility, suicidal thoughts, or convulsions. The damage to cognitive functioning can be so extreme, for example, that a person is unable to memorize something as simple as a phone number.

> **"I felt like my heart and head were beating fast.**
> **It only lasted a couple of minutes. Sometimes**
> **afterwards I'd get a pounding in my head."**
>
> —a thirteen-year-old girl who abused inhalants

Other physical damage includes optic nerve damage (resulting in partial blindness), hearing loss, liver damage, kidney failure, loss of bone marrow, muscle weakness and atrophy, limb spasms, numbness, digestive and respiratory problems, blood disorders, and heart irregularities. Because of the psychological, cognitive, and neurological damage, inhalant abusers present unique challenges in addiction treatment programs.[3]

Several things distinguish inhalant abuse from the abuse of other substances. First, the supply is limitless. These are common products found in almost every home. Products that can be used in this manner are so numerous that it would be impractical and unfeasible to try to eliminate or limit them. Although forty states have laws prohibiting the sale of some of these products to minors, they are rarely enforced.

Second, the problem rarely reaches the point of public awareness, and typically only in the wake of a tragic death. Many medical and education professionals, parents, and employers are not trained to identify the warning signs and symptoms of abuse. Students can be exposed to these substances in schools in art and industrial technology classes. Dentists, anesthesiologists, painters, and air-conditioning repair people also use these products occupationally. But the inability to identify signs of abuse means that users often go undetected, and they don't get the help they need early on.

Third, death can result even from first-time use. Sudden Sniffing Death Syndrome is the most common cause of death among inhalant abusers.[4] It happens when a user is surprised and the surge of adrenaline released by the brain to an already overstimulated, oxygen-deficient heart proves fatal. The startle response causes an abnormal pumping of the heart that leads to heart failure and sudden death. It can be precipitated by something as simple as a mother entering her son's bedroom and asking, "What are you doing?"

Finally, inhalant and solvent abuse results in profound, permanent, irreversible brain and nervous system damage. This is not the case with most other drugs of abuse.

Critical parts of the brain are literally dissolved, and functioning can never be restored.

Primary User Groups

As many as 16.7 million Americans have tried inhalants at least once in their lifetime, 7.5% of the total population over age twelve.[5] Inhalant abuse often starts early, and as with other drugs, as dependence develops the user seeks isolation. There are an estimated 622,000 current users (0.3%), with the highest rate among twelve to seventeen year-olds (1%).[6]

Among students, eighth graders have the highest rates of lifetime use (17.1%) and current use (4%).[7] Unlike many other drugs of abuse, the abuse of inhalants diminishes with age and is less prevalent among older versus younger teens. Current use is reported by only 1.7% of high school seniors.

Hospital emergencies for inhalants totaled 1,522 in 2000, down from 2,225 in 1997.[8] Inhalants are seldom the primary drug of abuse for persons seeking addiction treatment. In 1999 people reporting inhalants as the primary substance problem accounted for only 0.1% of all admissions, which was half as many as in 1994.[9] Of the inhalant-related admissions to addiction treatment programs, 54% were people under the age of twenty, and 19% were between the ages of twenty and twenty-nine.

The average age was 23.2 years. Males accounted for 72% and females 28%.[10]

Recent Developments

Hundreds of products abused in this manner produce long-term and damaging effects, and yet inhalant abuse barely registers on the public radar screen.[11]

Continuing Need for Effective Public Education

We minimize the problem of inhalant abuse every time we inhale helium from a balloon to make our voices change to a high pitch. When we show our kids how fun that is, we're teaching them that inhaling gas is funny, not dangerous. As a society we tend not to take inhalant abuse very seriously.

Education is the key to effective prevention and social change. We must all become more knowledgeable about the dangers of even onetime use of these toxins. We must learn how to communicate that danger to our children, not necessarily in the context of drug abuse, but in the same manner we point out the dangers of drinking contaminated water, breathing polluted air, or eating fish with high mercury levels. Poisons are harmful. Don't fool around with them, even a little bit. They can make you stupid, permanently. They can kill you.

Sniffers deliberately expose themselves to toxic chemicals and define the experience of their brain dissolving as pleasurable. If they realized what was actually producing the effects, most users might find it less pleasurable. Because use begins at such a young age, many users simply do not realize the extent of permanent damage they are inflicting. If they did, would they be less inclined to do it?

Inhalants are not drugs, they're poisons. They more closely resemble Agent Orange, DDT or other pesticides, and nuclear waste than marijuana, cocaine, or heroin. Yet when we insist that inhalant abuse education be part of the core curriculum of drug education classes for children, we may inadvertently teach our kids to identify them as potential recreational drugs. When drug education class teachers deliver lectures about inhalants, are they in effect instructing kids about how to do it?

It's a difficult issue. Clearly education is needed about the dangers of inhalant abuse. But we need to give deliberate consideration to the context of the educational message. Inhalant abuse prevention experts recommend teaching the dangers of exposure to solvents in various parts of the curriculum, not *just* during the drug education class. The dangers of inhalants should also be part of science classes, health classes, and secondary school discussions about environmental contaminants. Basic safety classes taught to elementary school students should incorporate the key message that smelling some things can hurt you.

Figure 21

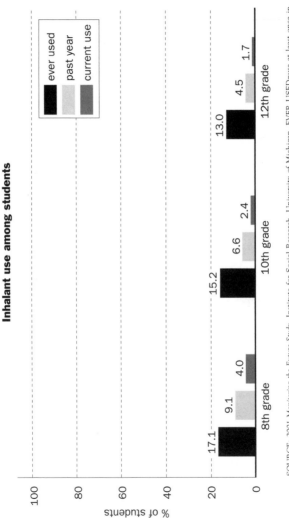

Inhalant use among students

SOURCE: 2001 *Monitoring the Future Study*, Institute for Social Research, University of Michigan. EVER USED=use at least once in lifetime. PAST YEAR=any use in the past year. CURRENT USE=any use in the past month.

Again, inhalant abuse is deliberate exposure to toxic chemicals. But when even the most well-intentioned educators tell kids that inhalants are another way to get high, kids turn these toxins into drugs, drugs they can easily find in the bathroom, in the garage, or under the kitchen sink. The critical challenge is to change the context and frame of reference of inhalant abuse education, to call it what it really is, and to deliver the message in places other than just drug education class.

"I haven't been to a school yet that gave information about inhalants. I never thought about the physical damage. I just didn't know. And when I found out here in treatment what inhalants can do to your brain, I thought, 'No way! I couldn't have been doing that to myself!' If I knew what inhalants could do, I never would have started.

"I'm worried now that I might have [continuing] brain damage. I get a lot of headaches. And sometimes things happen—like the other day I was at work counting chicken pieces in boxes. All I had to do was scan each box to see if a certain number was in there. I couldn't do it. I've always been really good at math, but I couldn't do a quick count of the chicken pieces in the box."

—an eighteen-year-old boy who'd been abusing fabric and leather protectors since age fourteen

12. Marijuana

Observable Indications of Use	Smell of marijuana smoke on breath and clothes Bloodshot eyes Talkativeness Inappropriate laughter Dry mouth Dilated pupils
Effects of Use	Enhanced sensory perception Relaxed state of well-being Impaired attention and short-term memory Impaired motor coordination Increased appetite Slowed internal clock Increased heart rate Increased blood pressure
Duration of Effects	2–3 hours
Signs of Overdose	Anxiety Extreme drowsiness Slurred speech Acute panic reaction
Fatal Overdose Possible	Unknown

Marijuana refers to the leaves and flowering tops of the hemp (cannabis) plant. It is also known as cannabis, bud, smoke, chronic, herb, reefer, pot, weed, ganja, or dope. The state of intoxication on marijuana is known as being high, loaded, baked, roasted, buzzed, or stoned. Sinsemilla ("without seed" in Spanish) is a type of high-potency marijuana. Ditch weed, commercial grade, and skunk weed refer to low-potency marijuana. Adolescents known to smoke marijuana are sometimes referred to as "stoners."

"[Smoking marijuana] was fun, though. And then it just became habitual. You know, it was beyond the point of enjoying it. It was enjoying me."

— a sixteen-year-old boy,
former marijuana abuser

Marijuana is smoked in hand-rolled cigarettes called joints or in hollowed-out cigars called blunts (named after a certain type of cigar). It is also smoked in small pipes known as one-hitters or tooters, or in a larger water pipe called a bong. Marijuana smoke is inhaled and held in the lungs as long as possible in order to maximize the effects. Marijuana can also be mixed into food and eaten or brewed with hot water into tea.

Although sixty cannabinoids (certain chemical compounds) are found in marijuana, the psychoactive one that most affects the brain is THC (delta-9-tetrahydrocannabinol). The THC level in marijuana has increased over the last quarter century. According to the U.S. Drug Enforcement Administration, the average THC content of marijuana in 1974 was less than 1%, compared with 5% in 1997. Due to advances in growing high-potency marijuana, some marijuana analyzed in 1997 had THC levels as high as 17%.[1]

THC is also produced synthetically and available by prescription (Marinol). The prescription medication is used to control the nausea caused by chemotherapy in cancer patients and to stimulate appetite in AIDS patients.

Hashish and hash oil also come from the cannabis plant. Hashish is a resinous material that is extracted and pressed into different shapes (balls, sheets, chunks). Smaller pieces are then broken off and smoked in a pipe. The average THC content of hashish in the United States is 6%. Hash oil is a dark-colored, gummy liquid that averages 15% THC content. It is smoked in a water pipe or by putting a few drops on a cigarette or joint.[2]

Effects and Consequences of Use

The effects of marijuana are subtler and less noticeable than the effects of many other drugs. A person under the influence may not be as easily recognized as such, compared with someone who is drunk on alcohol, tweaking on methamphetamine, or nodding on opiates. The effects peak within twenty minutes and last two or three hours.

Marijuana affects the parts of the brain involved in attention, memory, learning, and the integration of sensory experiences with motivation and emotions.[3] Marijuana intoxication impairs driving skills because it diminishes reaction time, motor coordination, and the ability to maintain and shift attention.[4] An adverse reaction to marijuana resembles a panic or anxiety attack.

Chronic marijuana use, like cigarette use, results in respiratory problems such as nagging coughs, frequent chest colds, chronic bronchitis, and increased risk of pneumonia. Scientific evidence indicates that long-term marijuana use can adversely affect the immune system and reproductive systems.[5]

Marijuana smoke contains some of the same cancer-causing agents that are in tobacco smoke. In fact, the tar and carbon monoxide levels absorbed by marijuana smokers are three to five times greater than those absorbed by tobacco smokers.[6] Smoking five joints per week exposes users to as many carcinogens as smoking a pack of cigarettes per day.

Both tolerance and mild withdrawal effects have been noted.[7] THC produces the same patterns of biochemical events that reinforce dependence on other drugs like cocaine and heroin.[8] Cannabis abuse and cannabis dependence are diagnostic categories for substance abuse disorder defined by the American Psychiatric Association.[9] A person is considered addicted if he or she compulsively and uncontrollably uses, craves, and seeks drugs, even in the face of repeated negative health and social consequences.

In 1999 nearly a quarter of a million Americans (223,597) sought addiction treatment with marijuana as the primary substance problem.[10]

Primary User Groups

An estimated 76.3 million Americans have tried marijuana/hashish at least once. But the number of current marijuana users has declined. In 2000, current marijuana use was reported by less than half as many people as twenty years earlier. Almost eleven million Americans (4.8%) used marijuana/hashish in the past month in 2000, compared with an estimated twenty-four million (13.2%) in 1979. (Most people who report use of marijuana/hashish use only marijuana.)[11]

Current marijuana use is most prevalent among people age eighteen to twenty-five (13.6%) and least prevalent among people over thirty-five (2.3%).[12] Marijuana use among youth age twelve to seventeen doubled from 1992 to 1995, from 3.4% to 8.2%. Since then it has declined to the 7.2% level.

Marijuana use among students increased in the 1990s, following a gradual decline since 1979. Its use increased

Figure 22

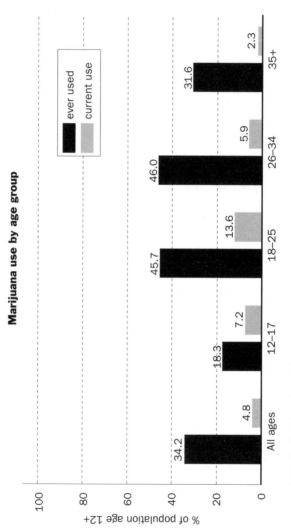

Marijuana use by age group

ever used
current use

% of population age 12+

	All ages	12–17	18–25	26–34	35+
ever used	34.2	18.3	45.7	46.0	31.6
current use	4.8	7.2	13.6	5.9	2.3

SOURCE: *2000 National Household Survey on Drug Abuse*, U.S. Department of Health and Human Services, Substance Abuse and Mental Health Services Administration, Office of Applied Studies, 2001. EVER USED=any use in lifetime. CURRENT USE=any use in past month.

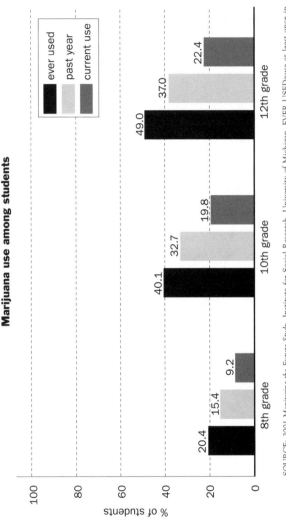

Figure 23

Marijuana use among students

- ever used
- past year
- current use

8th grade
- 20.4
- 15.4
- 9.2

10th grade
- 40.1
- 32.7
- 19.8

12th grade
- 49.0
- 37.0
- 22.4

% of students

SOURCE: *2001 Monitoring the Future Study*, Institute for Social Research, University of Michigan. EVER USED=use at least once in lifetime. PAST YEAR=any use in past year. CURRENT USE=any use in past month.

175

Figure 24

Marijuana-related hospital emergencies and treatment admissions by year

treatment admissions

hospital emergencies

thousands

240
200
160
120
80
40
0

1995 1996 1997 1998 1999 2000

SOURCE: Substance Abuse and Mental Health Services Administration, *Drug Abuse Warning Network*, Preliminary Estimates January–June 2001 with Revised Estimates 1994–2000, DHHS publication no. (SMA) 02-3634, and *Treatment Episode Date Set: 1994-1999*, DHHS publication no. (SMA) 01-3550.

in the 1990s and into the new millennium across all grade levels.[13] In 2001, almost one-quarter (22.4%) of high school seniors reported current marijuana use compared with 19.8% of tenth graders and 9.2% of eighth graders.

———

"When I was young, I vowed that I'd always be a marijuana smoker. But once I hit forty, smoking marijuana and even drinking one glass of alcohol just made me tired. So I very rarely do either anymore."

— a former heavy marijuana user

Marijuana use among high school seniors rose from 12% in 1992 to 22.4% in 2001. During that same time period (1992 to 2001) current use among tenth graders rose from 8% to 19.8%, and among eighth graders from 4% to 9.2%.[14]

Marijuana, while typically not the single drug that precipitates a visit to the hospital emergency room, appears in hospital emergency room data because abusers often use it at the same time they use other illegal drugs. (Each single drug-abuse-related episode tracks the "mention" of up to four possible drugs.)

Hospital emergencies involving marijuana doubled from 1995 to 2000.[15] Hospital emergencies rose from 45,000 in 1995 to 96,000 in 2000, and account for 16% of all drug-related hospital emergencies.

Marijuana treatment admissions also jumped during

these years—from 171,201 in 1995 to 223,597 in 1999. Marijuana accounted for 10.5% of total treatment admissions in 1995 and 14.1% in 1999.[16]

Nearly half (47.1%) of the marijuana-related admissions to addiction treatment programs in 1999 were people under the age of twenty.[17] The average age was 23.1 years. Males accounted for 77% and females 23%.[18]

Recent Developments

Marijuana Combined with Other Drugs

Marijuana is sometimes used in combination with other drugs of abuse and as a delivery medium for other drugs. Crack, psilocybin mushrooms, ketamine, or PCP are sometimes added to a marijuana joint. The slang names for the combinations vary considerably across different parts of the country. Joints with crack are sometimes known as geek joints, primos, turbos, or fireweed. Joints or blunts that contain PCP are known as love boats, honey-dipped joints, happy sticks, sherms, or dust blunts.[19]

Many users believe that dipping joints, even in substances that themselves would not be used as drugs of abuse, enhances the effects of the marijuana and makes the joints and blunts burn longer.[20] Some joints are dipped in formaldehyde, a key constituent of embalming fluid, or formaldehyde mixed with PCP.[21] Joints dipped in either formaldehyde alone or formaldehyde combined with PCP are known as fry, amp, dank, water-water, or wets. The PCP combination in particular is known to produce aggressive behavior in the users. Adolescent gang members sometimes refer to getting "amped up" before going out on a crime spree.

These variations make marijuana smoking even more unpredictable, particularly to unsuspecting novice users, who are led to believe the effects will be subtle and mild. Many users recall at least one bad experience (anxiety and panic reactions) after smoking joints that were laced with something.

"[M]ost people don't know what life is going to be day to day, but when you're a pothead you know what life is going to be day to day. It's like you have a goal. You have your mission and that's to get high. And now that I'm sober, I don't have a goal anymore. I don't have an interest in school, so that leaves me with no goal. I don't have my pot."

— a sixteen-year-old boy,
former marijuana abuser

420 (Four Twenty)

Among marijuana users, 4:20 is regarded as the univer-
sal time to get high. It's the exact time of day when
everyone who smokes marijuana should light up a joint.
It can be 4:20 A.M. or P.M. or both. April 20 (4/20) is a
special day, too. Pro-marijuana magazines sometimes
include a free 420 decal with every magazine purchased.
The 420 logo is also printed on T-shirts, hats, posters,
and backpacks, or written on the walls of middle schools,
high schools, and college campuses.

Indoor Marijuana-Growing Operations

Large quantities of marijuana enter the United States
from Mexico daily. For example, in 1997 more than 593
metric tons were seized on the U.S.-Mexican border.[22]
Marijuana is also grown domestically, and in recent years
many domestic growing operations have moved indoors.
This is partly because the grower can more easily fertil-
ize and tend the plants indoors, and partly in response
to efforts by law enforcement that detect and destroy
large outdoor growing operations. In 1998 the five leading states for indoor growing operations were California,
Alaska, Oregon, Kentucky, and Florida. Law enforcement
seized 2,616 indoor operations where growers cultivated
an average of eighty-nine plants.[23]

Vancouver, Canada, (home of BC Bud, a super-high-
potency marijuana) is the hot spot of marijuana-growing

expertise in North America. One retail store helps cus-
tomers set up an indoor growing operation in their homes.

Marijuana as Medicine

Opinions are sharply divided about the medical merits
of marijuana.[24] At the direction of the White House
Office of National Drug Control Policy, the Institute of
Medicine commissioned an independent panel of experts
to review the scientific literature regarding the health
benefits and deficits of marijuana and constituent
cannabinoids.[25]

The review, released in 1999, found that marijuana
components had modest therapeutic effects but that the
potential for their use as medicine was overridden by the
harm associated with smoke inhalation. The panel also
noted that for most conditions where marijuana's active
components may be helpful—pain, nausea, anorexia—
more effective medications already exist. It ruled out
marijuana as a treatment for glaucoma. The report under-
scored the preference for laboratory-produced cannabinoid
compounds for use in future research, because they are
quality-controlled and deliver a measurable, uniform dose.
The panel recommended further clinical trials.

Unprecedented policy changes on marijuana occurred
across the country in the late 1990s, as voters in California, Arizona, Oregon, Washington, Maine, Alaska,
Colorado, Nevada, and Washington, D.C., approved the

use of marijuana for medical reasons. These voter refer-endums created legal challenges to existing state and federal laws. Allowing an unapproved drug to be admin-istered to humans as medicine for health conditions flies in the face of the existing drug approval process.

"I heard [marijuana] was good health-wise but I
don't know how. I saw it in this *Time* magazine.
But I didn't really read the article. I saw this grandma
smoking it out of this pipe and stuff like that,
and eating it. People were eating it. Patients."

— a seventeen-year-old boy,
former marijuana abuser

Prescription and nonprescription drugs intended for human consumption undergo a rigorous approval process administered by the U.S. Food and Drug Administration (FDA). This assures American consumers that the drugs are safe, effective, and marketed in a manner that does not overstate the effects. This process was circumvented by voters in the 1990s, and these referendums represent uncharted waters on a number of fronts.

Hemp Products

Since the 1990s, various products made from hemp, the marijuana plant, are marketed to youthful consumers. The products range from shampoo to cooking oil to clothes to tennis shoes to jewelry. Movie stars and even governors openly promoted hemp.

Hemp refers to marijuana plants with low THC content, typically so low that the only effect from smoking it would be a headache. The only thing that distinguishes hemp from marijuana is THC content, which is discernable only by chemical analysis.

Decline in Disapproval and Perceived Harm of Marijuana Use

Marijuana use among youth began to rise in 1992 after a long period of gradual decline. Changing attitudes about the drug fueled the growth in its use. The Monitoring the Future Study found that when fewer students disapprove of marijuana use, marijuana use rises. And when fewer students believe marijuana is harmful, marijuana use rises.[26] These patterns were apparent in the 1990s when marijuana use increased at all grade levels.

To understand why marijuana use increased, consider the larger social, political, and cultural events that might have influenced adolescent perceptions about harm and disapproval: voters approved the medical use of marijuana, and hemp products were marketed to teens. What might these changes signify to adolescents?

To kids, medical marijuana initiatives may not be at all related to what they are for adults: compassionate treatment for the dying and suffering. Adolescents tend to think they are immortal anyway. Regardless of the message voters may be *trying* to send, the messages kids *receive* possibly boil down to this: (1) if marijuana is medicine, then it can't be harmful, and (2) adults must approve of marijuana because they voted for it.

Regardless of whether hemp's potential as a commercial crop is a well-advised business venture or folly, consider the message to youth. To the teenager, the possible message is this: Marijuana can't be *that* bad, because look at all the adults who want to grow it. Adults *must* approve of it or they wouldn't want to grow it.

This argument is intentionally simplistic. Clearly numerous factors influenced youth attitudes about the harm and disapproval of marijuana in the 1990s, especially the ambivalence of their baby-boom-generation parents about what, if anything, to tell their kids about it.

But perhaps no marijuana messages were more influential than those from the broader adult society. One marijuana message came from the public-policy arena and another from the consumer arena. People *voted* for medical marijuana. People *produced* things out of hemp. If we consider how actions speak louder than words, particularly adult actions and particularly to the young, it's perhaps no surprise that the 1990s was a decade of growing marijuana use among America's youth.

The consequences of this growth in marijuana use by

America's young are seen in the nation's treatment centers. Those who nostalgically cling to the notion that marijuana is not harmful and dismiss the claim that it's stronger now need only look at treatment centers to see the harm that comes from marijuana use by youth.

Almost 225,000 Americans sought addiction treatment in 1999, citing marijuana as their primary drug. Nearly half were under the age of twenty.

"My problems didn't seem to disappear when I was using marijuana, but they stopped hurting for a while. All of a sudden I was *part of,* not *apart from,* and they just—they made me feel really included. You don't have to be yourself when you're high. You could be something. And it's just an easier way to get all the pressure off of trying to act right, because when you're high, you don't have to act right."

— a sixteen-year-old girl,
former marijuana abuser

13. Methamphetamine/ Stimulants

Observable Indications of Use	Talkativeness High energy level/restlessness Dry mouth Dilated pupils Sores on skin from scratching at "crank bugs"
Effects of Use	Loss of appetite Increased mental alertness Increased physical energy Insomnia Paranoia Distorted perceptions (auditory and visual) Repetitive motor activity Sweating (at higher doses) Palpitations (at higher doses) Body tremors (at higher doses) Increased heart rate Elevated blood pressure MDMA: jaw tension, teeth grinding
Duration of Effects	Methamphetamine: 8–12 hours MDMA: 4–6 hours

Signs of Overdose	Convulsions
	Agitation
	MDMA: heat stroke, extreme elevation
	  in body temperature (hyperthermia),
	  dehydration

Fatal Overdose Possible	Yes, due to cardiac arrest or stroke from high blood pressure **IMPORTANT: If you suspect a person may have overdosed on methamphetamine/stimulants, call 911 and seek emergency medical treatment immediately.**

Types of Stimulants

Prescription Stimulants

Amphetamine is a general category of stimulants that includes amphetamine, dextroamphetamine, and methamphetamine.[1] The three types are so similar in terms of chemical composition and effects that most users cannot distinguish the difference. The prescription Dexedrine (brown and clears, dexes, beans) is dextroamphetamine. The prescriptions Benzedrine (bennies, black beauties) and Adderall are amphetamines. These are prescribed in the treatment of narcolepsy and obesity, and among children for attention disorders. *Methylphenidate* is a pharmaceutical stimulant prescribed to reduce excessive daytime sleepiness in persons with narcolepsy (Provigil) and in the medical treatment of ADHD (attention-deficit hyperactivity disorder) (Ritalin, Methylin, Concerta). Used as prescribed for ADHD, methylphenidate calms hyperactivity and increases the ability of children to focus on tasks.[2]

Pediatricians write more than half of the amphetamine and methylphenidate prescriptions. The number of prescriptions written for ADHD has increased fivefold from 1991 to 1999. In 1999, eleven million prescriptions were written for methylphenidate and six million for Adderall.[3]

The rate of ADHD is extremely variable across communities. Some school districts have no students diagnosed with ADHD, while others report up to 20% of students, a variability that suggests the likelihood of improper diagnosis.[4] Whatever the case, such widespread medication of America's children remains very controversial.[5]

Methylphenidate has also emerged as a drug of abuse. Diversion of pharmaceutical methylphenidate is the only source of it available for abuse. It is stolen from school nurse offices, siblings, and other children with ADHD. Some patients with ADHD readily give it to their classmates, calling them "hyper pills." Sometimes they or their siblings sell the pills or trade them for other drugs such as marijuana. Methylphenidate is among the pharmaceutical drugs most frequently stolen from licensed handlers and is also diverted through scams, forgeries, and doctor shopping.

As a drug of abuse, it is sought after for its stimulant effects and euphoria. It is crushed and snorted intranasally, or dissolved in water and the mixture injected. Injectable methylphenidate in Chicago is known as "west coast." It is also mixed with heroin to make an injectable "speedball." The danger of injection is that complications often arise from the insoluble fillers used in its manufacture, which block blood vessels and cause damage to the retina of the eyes and the lungs.[6]

The 1999 Monitoring the Future Study reported that 3% of high school seniors had used methylphenidate nonmedically in the past year. There were 1,727 hospital emergency room episodes involving methylphenidate in 1998; more than half involved patients age ten through seventeen.[7]

Other Stimulants

Methcathinone, also known as cat, is a combination of methamphetamine and cathinone. It is most often produced in clandestine labs and abused in a manner similar to methamphetamine. *Khat* is a plant used in East Africa and Arabia (chewed or brewed in tea) for its stimulant properties. Its two active ingredients are controlled substances in the United States, however: cathinone and cathine.

Methamphetamine

Methamphetamine is a stimulant that is synthetically produced in clandestine labs and closely resembles amphetamine in molecular structure and effects. Methamphetamine is also known as meth, crank, crystal, crystal meth, and speed. Methamphetamine is a white powder that is snorted, smoked, or injected intravenously. It can also be pressed into pills and taken orally. Depending on the method and ingredients used to manufacture methamphetamine, it can have a white, off-white, brown, purple, yellowish, pinkish, reddish, or pale green color. Smokable methamphetamine, known as glass or ice, is smoked by inhaling the vapors.[8]

MDMA (Ecstasy)

MDMA (3,4-methylenedioxymethamphetamine) is a methamphetamine with hallucinogenic properties (see page 125). MDMA is also known as Ecstasy, X, XTC, Adam, or E. Because it allegedly enhances tactile sensations and sexual pleasure, MDMA is also known as the "hug drug" or "love drug." It is sold and used at rave parties, concerts, and nightclubs.

People under the influence of MDMA are said to be "rolling," although this term also applies to youth taking a combination of drugs in a party or rave setting. MDMA users also engage in body massages or sometimes wear disposable surgical masks rubbed with mentholated cold preparations that supposedly heighten the effects of the drug. Users may also use oral pacifiers to reduce teeth grinding and relieve jaw tension, a side effect of MDMA.[9] Glow sticks are also used to increase sensory input.

MDMA is a white powder that is pressed into small pills that come in various pastel colors. The pills have

"I used to work nights, and that's what really got me started. My boss had it all the time on the night shift and he'd give me a line. After work I'd go home and I couldn't sleep. Come back the next day tired and had no choice but to do another line."

— a meth user

different symbols, corporate logos, or shapes imprinted into them, such as a butterfly, four-leaf clover, or happy face. They are taken orally.

The effects, which last four to six hours, include both feelings of deep relaxation and stimulant effects that allow the user to dance for hours on end and party until dawn. MDMA has amphetamine-like stimulant effects combined with mescaline-like hallucinogenic effects. Signs of overdose are elevated heartbeat, elevated blood pressure, sweating, dehydration, elevated body temperature, cramping, panic attacks, and possible seizures or loss of consciousness.

Because MDMA elevates the body temperature, many raves have "chill-out rooms" where users can take a break by being in air-conditioning or taking a cold shower. The U.S. Drug Enforcement Administration reports core body temperatures among MDMA-related decedents as high as 109 degrees.[10]

MDMA use is also dangerous because not all pills sold as Ecstasy actually contain MDMA. See page 204 under "Recent Developments" (in this chapter).

The U.S. Drug Enforcement Administration (DEA) reports significant increases in seizures of MDMA entering the United States from Europe. In 2000 the DEA estimated that as many as two million tablets are smuggled into the United States every week.[11]

Effects and Consequences of Use

The effects are felt within several minutes after methamphetamine is snorted, almost immediately after injection, and twenty minutes after oral ingestion. The intense rush, or euphoric feeling, experienced as the drug reaches the brain can last up to twenty minutes. Initially the user appears alert, more attentive, and even euphoric. The effects are increased energy levels, alertness, and loss of appetite that last eight to twelve hours. Tolerance develops after repeated use, as the body requires more of the drug to achieve the desired effect.

Methamphetamine users are prone to go on binges, sometimes lasting for up to two weeks, during which time they keep taking the drug but do not eat or sleep. Chronic use results in significant weight loss. Because it suppresses fatigue and appetite, profound physical deterioration can be more noticeable among meth addicts than other drug abusers.

The user may experience mood disturbances and at times exhibit outbursts of aggression. During long binges, paranoid delusions may develop, also known as methamphetamine psychosis. The user may believe, for example, that people are "after me" or "out to get me." A user may spend hours looking out the window, absolutely convinced that the police are in the front yard watching, only to later realize that what was so worrisome was not a person but a shrub. Users may imagine that people ("shadow people") follow them around, or they may experience auditory hallucinations.

While under the influence of methamphetamine, users can lose track of time or engage in repetitive, pointless activities like cleaning the bathroom floor tiles with a toothbrush, fixing things that weren't broken, or cutting the lawn with a scissors. Other compulsive behaviors might include picking at their skin and creating open sores and lesions or scratching at imaginary "crank bugs." "Tweaking" occurs near the end of a binge cycle when users realize that nothing they can do will diminish their discomfort, not even taking more of the drug.[12] Users often turn to depressant drugs like alcohol or opiates to relieve the discomfort. The binge is followed by a crash period lasting one to three days. This is a period of fatigue, prolonged sleep, intense craving for the drug, and possible depression.

The effects of long-term methamphetamine abuse and addiction strongly resemble the psychiatric diagnosis of paranoia or paranoid schizophrenia. As a result, methamphetamine addicts are not always immediately identified

"With meth I went for days and didn't have to worry about where to sleep or eat."

— a formerly homeless teenage girl

as drug abusers, particularly when they ask for help at a psychiatric hospital or clinic. Because one of the ingredients in homemade methamphetamine recipes is lead acetate, some chronic users, particularly injectors, also suffer from acute lead poisoning.[13]

With most other drugs of abuse, the brain function returns to the normal state after the drug use is terminated, usually within weeks or months, depending on the amount and duration of abuse. But scientific evidence suggests more lasting effects from prolonged methamphetamine abuse. Animal studies show that after repeated exposure to fairly small amounts of methamphetamine, more than half of the actual brain cells that produce a certain chemical messenger (neurotransmitter) are damaged. Methamphetamine is a neurotoxin.[14]

Recent research indicates that MDMA also damages, perhaps irreparably, certain parts of the brain that produce necessary chemical messengers. These findings suggest that MDMA users risk permanent brain damage that can manifest behaviorally in anxiety, depression, or other psychiatric disorders.[15]

Primary User Groups

Because it prolongs wakefulness and reduces fatigue, methamphetamine is used by people who want to accomplish more tasks such as household chores, work, sports, dancing, or social activities. Methamphetamine is used by employees, mothers, party-goers, or students who want to fight fatigue, by athletes seeking to enhance athletic performance, and by dieters for its appetite-suppressant effects.

In 2000 an estimated 8.8 million Americans had tried methamphetamine at least once (4% of the U.S. population age twelve and older).[16] Current use was reported by 0.3% of twelve to seventeen and eighteen to twenty-five-year-olds. Methamphetamine use among students in 2001 was reported by 1.3% of eighth graders, 1.5% of tenth graders, and 1.5% of high school seniors.

Ecstasy use in the past month was reported by 1.8% of eighth graders, 2.6% of tenth graders, and 2.8% of high school seniors. Almost 12% of seniors, 8% of tenth graders, and 5.2% of eighth graders had tried it at least once.[17]

Nationwide, hospital emergency department episodes and treatment admissions involving methamphetamine increased throughout the 1990s.

Hospital emergencies from MDMA rose 58% from 1999 to 2000, with 4,511 that year. See also figure 17 on page 130. Hospital emergencies for methamphetamine declined slightly from 1995 to 2000, yet amphetamine mentions rose to create an overall net increase, with 30,639 combined mentions in 2000.[18]

Figure 25

Nonmedical use of stimulants by age group

% of population age 12+

| ever used | current use |

| All ages | 12–17 | 18–25 | 26–34 | 35+ |

6.6 0.4 — All ages
4.0 0.8 — 12–17
7.6 0.8 — 18–25
6.8 0.4 — 26–34
6.7 0.2 — 35+

SOURCE: 2000 National Household Survey on Drug Abuse, U.S. Department of Health and Human Services, Substance Abuse and Mental Health Services Administration, Office of Applied Studies, 2001. EVER USED=any use in lifetime. CURRENT USE=any use in past month. This refers only to the nonmedical use of any prescription-type stimulant and does not include over-the-counter drugs.

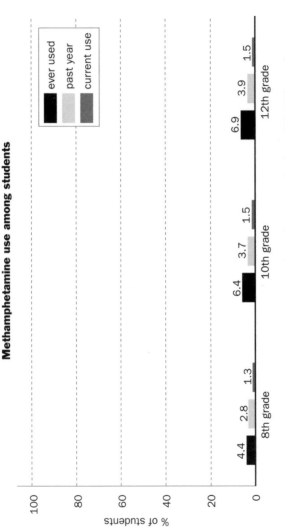

Figure 26

Methamphetamine use among students

ever used
past year
current use

8th grade
4.4   2.8   1.3

10th grade
6.4   3.7   1.5

12th grade
6.9   3.9   1.5

% of students

0   20   40   60   80   100

SOURCE: *2001 Monitoring the Future Study*, Institute for Social Research, University of Michigan. EVER USED=use at least once in lifetime. PAST YEAR=any use in past year. CURRENT USE=any use in past month.

Figure 27

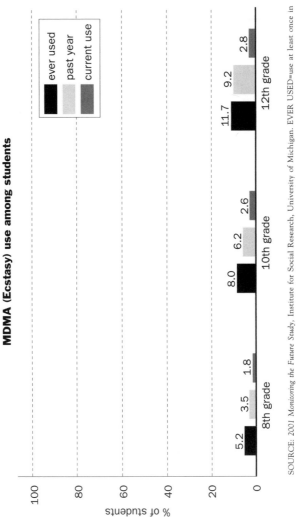

MDMA (Ecstasy) use among students

SOURCE: *2001 Monitoring the Future Study*, Institute for Social Research, University of Michigan. EVER USED=use at least once in lifetime. PAST YEAR=any use in past year. CURRENT USE=any use in past month.

Figure 28

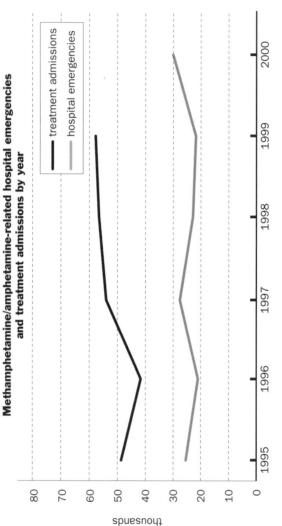

Methamphetamine/amphetamine-related hospital emergencies and treatment admissions by year

SOURCE: Substance Abuse and Mental Health Services Administration, Drug Abuse Warning Network, Preliminary Estimates, January–June 2001 with Revised Estimates 1994-2000, DHHS publication no. (SMA) 02-3634, and *Treatment Episode Data Set: 1994–1999*, DHHS publication no. (SMA) 01-3550.

From 1995 to 1999 treatment admissions for methamphetamine increased from 47,837 to 57,834 and represent 3.6% of all treatment admissions. Males accounted for 53% of admissions and females 47%. Only 9.2% of the methamphetamine-related admissions to addiction treatment programs were people under the age of twenty. The average age at admission was 30.6 years.[19] Using existing data systems, it is not yet possible to separate out MDMA admissions to treatment.

Recent Developments

Methamphetamine is a drug that has taken hold largely in rural areas of the country. Home cookers of meth have increased, and, although meth has now started appearing to a very small extent in some East Coast urban nightclub scenes, its origins and popularity reside in rural and urban areas of the West Coast, Southwest, and Midwest.

Influx of Methamphetamine from Mexico

Most methamphetamine consumed in the United States is produced in and imported from Mexico. The amounts entering the United States from Mexico recently increased significantly. In 1998 U.S. law enforcement agents along the Mexican border seized 560 kilograms of methamphetamine, compared with only 6.5 kilograms in 1992.[20]

For many years methamphetamine abuse and distribution

were largely confined to motorcycle gangs operating out of the southwestern areas of the United States. But now, due in part to increased difficulty in acquiring precursor chemicals in the United States, Mexican-produced methamphetamine has overtaken the U.S. market. The criminal networks and Mexican "families" experienced in the wholesale distribution of cocaine have now added methamphetamine to their repertoire. As a result, methamphetamine use and distribution networks are expanding to other regions of the country.

Clandestine Rural Meth Labs

Smaller-scale entrepreneurs try to produce smaller amounts of methamphetamine themselves in makeshift do-it-yourself labs. These are typically methamphetamine users who have no particular background or training in chemistry. Meth lab operators, like users, tend to be young, white, blue-collar males.

The number of meth labs dismantled nationally by the U.S. Drug Enforcement Administration increased from 224 in 1994 to 1,627 in 1998. Midwestern states in particular have seen large increases in meth lab activity in recent years.

Clandestine meth labs typically operate in remote rural areas, where the strong chemical fumes are less detectable. One methamphetamine lab in Minnesota was located out on a frozen lake inside an ice-fishing shack. But meth labs are also located in more populated areas or high-density housing units like apartment buildings or motel rooms. This increases the risk of potential harm to innocent people when the fumes are carried through centralized heating or ventilation systems.

Makeshift labs have the capacity to create a small batch of methamphetamine in several hours without elaborate equipment. Ingredients include over-the-counter ephedrine-based products combined with other readily accessible compounds, such as those found in batteries and used in farming. The by-products generated during and after manufacture are also hazards to nearby people (who may breathe the fumes) and surrounding property (causing soil and water contamination). Because the ingredients are caustic and volatile, there is a high risk of explosion and flash fire. Additionally, the cookers are not trained chemists and so do not know what remedial steps to take when the recipe goes wrong. Children living in homes where the adults are making meth have required emergency medical treatment for exposure to the toxic chemicals and fumes.

The manufacture of every unit of finished product of methamphetamine produces six or seven units of by-products and hazardous waste. The residual fumes, equipment, waste, and by-products are so toxic that law enforcement agents now routinely use hazardous-material protective gear and handling procedures. The cleanup of a small lab can cost up to $30,000. Larger labs cost even more.

Ecstasy—Not Just at Nightclubs Anymore

While MDMA (Ecstasy) was initially categorized as a "club drug" due to its sale and abuse at nightclubs and raves, its use and distribution now extends beyond those settings. Wherever adolescents and young adults live, go to school, or congregate, Ecstasy is not far away. Distribution and abuse are increasingly prevalent, particularly in affluent, suburban areas.

If It's a Pill, It Must Be Safe

In this age of scientific advancement, medications are being developed and ingested to prevent illness, treat disease, and promote health. Millions of school-age children take daily medication for a variety of behavioral and medical disorders. Prescription and over-the-counter drugs are heavily advertised in print and broadcast media. Indeed, most Americans take some sort of vitamin, supplement, over-the-counter, or prescription medication on a regular basis.

Consequently, many young people believe that any type of pill must be at least somewhat "safe" and "legitimate," even pills sold as Ecstasy. Many users dismiss the actual risk of Ecstasy use and cavalierly say, "It's just a pill," implying minimal, if any, risk. Despite this nonchalant attitude, the unknown origin and content of the pills continue to pose a very real danger.

Ecstasy Knockoffs, Variations, and Combinations

Laboratory analysis of pills and capsules continues to reveal that not all pills sold as Ecstasy actually contain MDMA. Some pills contain PMA (para-methoxyamphetamine) and PMMA (para-methoxymethamphetamine), more potent forms of MDMA. Some pills contain PCP, AMT, MDX, ephedrine, methamphetamine, or ketamine only. BZP and TFMPP, both piperazine-based compounds, have also been sold as Ecstasy. Piperazine is used in veterinary medicine as a dewormer. 5-MeO-DIPT, a hallucinogen known as *Foxy* or *Methoxy Foxy*, has also been sold as Ecstasy. The list of chemical compounds will continue to grow as unscrupulous people purchase "research chemicals" on the Internet and use them to produce Ecstasy knockoffs—pills or capsules that are falsely sold as MDMA-containing Ecstasy.

Other chemical variations that combine the effects of amphetamines and mescaline include compounds such as STP ("serenity, tranquility, and peace"); DOB (4-bromo-2-,5-dimethoxyamphetamine); and 2C-B or Nexus. Nexus is typically sold under its own name, however.

Use of multiple doses of MDMA and using it in combination with other pills is becoming a more frequent occurrence. "Stacking" refers to taking three or more pills at once. "Piggy backing" refers to taking a series of pills sequentially in a short period of time, also known as a "trail mix approach." "Totem poles" are pills piled on top of one another taken sequentially or simultaneously. "Candy flipping" refers to the simultaneous use of MDMA and LSD. And "sextasy" refers to the simultaneous use of Viagra and Ecstasy, most often reported in aging, gay communities.

14. Sedatives/Hypnotics

Observable Indications of Use	Slurred speech Drunken-like behavior with no smell of alcohol Clumsiness Drowsiness Droopy eyes Dilated pupils
Effects of Use	Sedation Reduced anxiety Lowered blood pressure Slowed pulse
Duration of Effects	Barbiturates: 4–16 hours Tranquilizers: 4–12 hours Methaqualone: 4–8 hours Flunitrazepam: 4–8 hours Gamma hydroxybutyrate: 3–6 hours
Signs of Overdose	Shallow, slow breathing Cold, clammy skin Fast, weak pulse Coma Seizure-like actions (for GHB, GBL)
Fatal Overdose Possible	Yes, from respiratory arrest and especially when used in combination with other depressant drugs, including alcohol **IMPORTANT: If you suspect a person may have overdosed on sedatives/hypnotics, call 911 and seek emergency medical treatment immediately.**

Sedative/hypnotic drugs are used to produce sedation, induce sleep, or reduce anxiety.

Types of Sedatives/Hypnotics

This is a very large category of drugs that includes prescription sleeping medications, anticonvulsants, anti-anxiety medications, tranquilizing medications, and new synthetic depressant drugs. These prescription medications, when used as drugs of abuse, are known as downers or goofballs. They are taken orally or injected. This category includes barbiturates (Seconal, Phenobarbital, Nembutal, barbs); methaqualone (Quaaludes, ludes); and benzodiazepines (Valium, Librium, Klonopin, Ativan, Xanax). Barbiturates, due to their long duration of action, are not often seen as drugs of abuse. Methaqualone, or Quaaludes, once a popular drug of abuse in the 1970s, is rarely abused today.[1]

Several new drugs in this category appeared in the 1990s. These were quickly dubbed "date-rape drugs" for their use in drug-assisted rapes, but they are also knowingly ingested as drugs of abuse. They are flunitrazepam (Rohypnol), GHB (gamma hydroxybutyrate), and GHB analogs (GHB's chemical cousins, GBL, GVL, and 1,4-BD), which are sold as nutritional supplements, growth hormones, and cleaning solvents. These substances are among the fastest-growing drugs of abuse by young people today.

Flunitrazepam

Flunitrazepam (Rohypnol), a long-acting benzodiazepine, is also known as roofies, roach pills, Mexican Valium, or rope. It is up to ten times stronger than Valium. Although not approved for medical use in the United States, it is used medically in many other countries to treat insomnia.

Flunitrazepam also produces amnesia-like effects. People under its influence experience a state similar to an alcoholic blackout: they are conscious, walking, and talking but later have no recall of what transpired. The effects of flunitrazepam appear within twenty minutes of administration and last four to eight hours.[2] Victims who have unknowingly been given the drug report being overtaken by a very heavy, drugged feeling that makes it difficult to lift their limbs and even stay awake. They feel sluggish, and some report residual hangover-like effects well into the next day or even two.

Some young people at rave parties and nightclubs use Rohypnol and GHB as drugs of abuse to produce a drunken-like state. Worse, the drugs are also used in a predatory way to sedate people in order to harm or sexually assault them. Rohypnol and GHB are sometimes

"Drugs are not just for people who knowingly
take them anymore. They are used . . .
to disable victims and render them helpless."

used to facilitate violent crime when they are placed in beverages of people (without their knowledge) who, once sedated, are raped and assaulted.

Since 1985, the U.S. Drug Enforcement Administration has documented more than 4,500 federal, state, and local law enforcement cases involving flunitrazepam in thirty-eight states.[3]

It is very difficult to ascertain how often Rohypnol is used in drug-assisted rapes and assaults. Coming forward to report a rape or sexual assault is difficult enough without the added dimension of having no memory of it. But since flunitrazepam is detectable in urine for up to seventy-two hours after ingestion, women who suspect they may have been exposed should seek the services of a sexual assault center as soon as possible.

GHB

GHB (gamma hydroxybutyrate), like flunitrazepam, is used in other countries in the treatment of sleep disorders; it has been recently approved for medical use in the United States by the product name Xyrem. GHB is also known as G, Great Hormones at Bedtime, Salty Water, Gamma, Liquid E, Liquid X, Grievous Bodily Harm, and Organic Quaalude. It is used in drug-assisted rapes and also promoted as an alleged muscle-stimulating growth hormone, sleep aid, and aphrodisiac. Being drugged then raped is known as being "scooped," and GHB used in this manner is sometimes known as "scoop." Other substances appearing with increasing frequency are similar in effect and chemical structure to GHB. These GHB analogs include GBL, also known as furanone di-hydro or gamma butyrolactone, and 1,4-butanediol, known as BD or 1,4-BD. Both are related to GHB and convert to GHB when ingested. GBL and 1,4-BD are also precursor chemicals that are used in the manufacture of GHB. GVL, gamma valerolactone or 4-pentanolide, is used as a GHB substitute because it metabolizes into GHV. GHV, gamma hydroxyvalerate or methyl-GHB, is a compound that produces GHB-like effects.

GHB and related compounds are drugs of abuse primarily among adolescents and young adults in their twenties. It is a white powder that is dissolved in beverages or a liquid sold in bottles or small vials. The liquid form has appeared in many different colors, including bright yellow, aqua, dark blue, red, and clear. Usually purchased in nightclubs and at parties, it is often combined with water in clear plastic bottles. A dose is administered by taking a swig from a bottle or small plastic bottle cap.[4]

> **"It's sad to say, but we live in a world where people actually do this to other people."**
>
> — a college student in reference to drug-assisted rape

The effects are felt within fifteen minutes and last three to six hours. In low doses GHB creates feelings of relaxation, slows breathing and heart rate, and affects balance and motor coordination. In higher doses deep sleep transpires. Users describe its effects as euphoric, restful, and refreshing. Adverse overdose reactions include vomiting, loss of consciousness, seizure-like activity, respiratory arrest, coma, and death. Tolerance and dependence are possible. Addicts have reported tremors, anxiety attacks, numbness in the extremities, and other neurological symptoms.

As of January 2000, the Drug Enforcement Administration documented more than 5,700 overdoses and law enforcement encounters with GHB in forty-five states, and sixty-five GHB-related deaths.[5]

Not all people who start using GHB or GHB analogs do so to achieve a high. To the contrary, some are motivated by health promotion. They may be introduced to it at a gym or fitness center as a supplement that can help them bulk up, for example. They may be completely unaware of the immediate health effects, the addictive potential, or the long-term consequences associated with regular use.

**"Knowing what I know now about GHB? There's no way
I would ever even TRY that stuff!"**

— a former GHB user whose friend was rushed to the
emergency room for a GHB adverse reaction

GHB-Involved Hospital Emergencies: 1995–2000

1995	145
1996	638
1997	762
1998	1,282
1999	3,178
2000	4,969

Source: Office of National Drug Control Policy (November 1999). Drug Abuse Warning Network, DAWN, 2002.

GHB hospital emergencies have increased significantly since 1995. See also figure 17 on page 130. Most episodes involve patients between the ages of eighteen and twenty-five. These figures underestimate the actual magnitude of GHB abuse, however, because cases are reportable on the data system only when a patient knowingly ingests a drug. Therefore, cases in which people are administered GHB without their knowledge (as in drug-facilitated rape cases) are *not* recorded. In addition, it is difficult to ascertain how many adverse health events are attributable to GHB itself or to the GHB-related analogs (GBL, 1,4-BD, GHV, and GVL). (See "Recent Developments," page 215.)

Effects and Consequences of Use

Drugs in this category are depressants that induce relaxed, sleepy states. Sleeping medications depress or slow down the central nervous system. This results in drowsiness, slurred speech, and drunken-like behavior. Signs of overdose include shallow breathing, clammy skin, rapid pulse, and coma. Fatal overdose can occur from depressed respiration. Because these are depressants, combining them with other depressant drugs like alcohol is extremely dangerous and can result in fatal coma.

Tolerance can develop with sedatives/hypnotics, especially after prolonged use. Particularly with benzodiazepines, discontinuation of use should be gradual and attempted only under medical supervision, since life-threatening seizures can occur during withdrawal.

Primary User Groups

An estimated 175,000 Americans age twelve and older (0.1%) reported the nonmedical use of sedatives in 2000, and one million (0.4%) reported the nonmedical use of tranquilizers.[6]

In 2001, 2.8% of high school seniors reported current use of barbiturates; 3.0% reported current use of tranquilizers. Only 1.6% of seniors reported GHB use in the past year.[7]

Benzodiazepines are a favored drug of abuse among narcotic addicts, taken to reduce the symptoms of chronic opiate use and in combination with opiates to prolong and enhance the effects. They are also used following a methamphetamine binge to "take the edge off" and facilitate rest.

More than 210,000 hospital emergencies were related to sedatives, hypnotics, and anxiolytics in 2000, 91,000 of which were benzodiazepines.[8]

Very few people receiving treatment report sedatives as the primary drug of abuse. In 1999, 0.3% of all admissions were for tranquilizers and 0.2% were for sedatives/hypnotics. Unlike any other drug, depressants are used more often by women than men. Women accounted for almost 60% of admissions for both tranquilizers and sedatives/hypnotics. The average age of admission was thirty-six years.[9] It is difficult to accurately estimate the number of GHB-addicted patients entering treatment.

Recent Developments

GHB and Related Compounds

Some compounds that quickly convert into GHB when ingested are sold in retail outlets and on the Internet as nutritional supplements and, more recently, cleaning solvents. The chemical names of the most commonly found compounds that when ingested convert to GHB are gamma butyrolactone (GBL) and 1,4-butanediol (BD).

The U.S. Food and Drug Administration (FDA) has issued multiple warnings on the GBL-containing products, including a voluntary recall of those sold in health food stores in 1999.[10] GBL is used industrially as a solvent in the polymer, pharmaceutical, and agriculture industries. It is also believed to be the primary precursor chemical used in the large-scale clandestine manufacture of GHB. And 1,4-butanediol has been declared a Class I Health Hazard. These chemicals, whether sold as nutritional supplements or solvents, pose significant health risks when ingested.

—

"I started using GHB to come down off of heroin. But after a while I was using it every three hours, every day, for three months. And even though I'd pass out and wake up in the emergency room, I just kept using it. If I didn't take it, I'd feel all sweaty and start to panic."

— a former GHB user

GBL-containing nutritional supplements are marketed for bodybuilding and weight loss and as sleep aids. They are sold on the Internet, in health food stores, and in gyms. One label on a bottle of a GBL-containing nutritional supplement stated that users would become unarousable and that "this is normal." The label also encouraged people to let users "sleep it off" and explicitly said *not* to call emergency medical personnel because they will perform "unnecessary and expensive medical procedures." Remember that GBL converts quickly into GHB, which can cause slowed respiration, loss of consciousness, seizures, vomiting, and death.

After the FDA recall of GBL products in January 1999

they became somewhat more difficult to find in stores and on the Internet. In August 1999, however, the FDA issued another warning about GHB, GBL, and BD, noting that some manufacturers had renamed the products and changed the product labeling.[11]

GBL-containing liquids have now surfaced on the Internet as cleaning solvents, nail polish remover, and even tropical fish tank cleaner. Other GHB analogs— 1,4-BD, GHV, or GVL—may be present in these products as well. And they can be labled as almost anything. Although the bottle labels state that the solvents are not intended for human consumption, some of the words used to describe the effects are similar to slang terms used to describe states of intoxication. GHB was added to the federal list of controlled substances in February 2000, but whether this will help curb the elusive marketing of GBL and other GHB-related analogs remains unclear.[12] Some products even make false claims that they do not contain GHB compounds when, in fact, they do.

What distinguishes the use of GHB and related products from the abuse of other illicit drugs of abuse is that some people who abuse them are not drug abusers seeking mood-altering effects. Some are hapless victims who consume these products in beverages without their knowledge and are subsequently raped, robbed, assaulted, or otherwise harmed. Still others are health enthusiasts who are introduced to these products at a health club or gym. Typically these users believe they are taking a helpful dietary supplement and blindly accept the bogus health claims written on the bottles or delivered by another user. They are unaware of the actual contents of the product or associated risks.

Drug-Assisted Rape

The predatory use of drugs to render people helpless so they cannot resist or recall a crime is a growing phenomenon. Girls as young as thirteen in urban and rural areas attend parties, whether or not they drink alcohol. Young women go to bars, clubs, restaurants, or bowling alleys. College students go to Florida, Texas, or Mexico for spring break. Because of the date-rape-drug phenomenon, they all now risk the real possibility of being unknowingly drugged and subsequently raped or assaulted.[13]

The personal stories of the women who have experienced drug-assisted sexual assault are horrific. Some were so drugged that the extreme altered state lasted for three days. Some awakened alone, beat up, violated, and naked in abandoned vehicles in remote areas, having no idea how they got there or what happened. Some recall a dreamlike state of drifting in and out of consciousness during a rape by multiple people.

Men drug women in order to rape them. Prostitutes drug johns in order to rob them. Drugs are not just for people who knowingly take them anymore. They are used in the commission of crimes to disable victims and render them helpless.

In response to the growing problem of drug-assisted rape, a federal law was enacted in 1996 that imposes penalties of up to twenty years for the use of Rohypnol and similar debilitating tranquilizers in the commission of a rape. It also imposes a three-year penalty for possession.

February 2000 marked the first criminal prosecution stemming from a GHB-related death. At a party in Detroit in 1999, two young girls consumed beverages that contained GHB that had been added without their knowledge. One girl awoke in a hospital bed hours later. The other girl, a fifteen-year-old, never regained consciousness and died of GHB poisoning. Three male defendants were charged and convicted of involuntary manslaughter and mixing a harmful substance in a drink.[14]

GHB was added to the federal list of controlled substances in February 2000, after twenty states had already done so. GHB was added to the category of drugs that carries the most severe penalties—those with no approved

---

"She had sex with all the guys and she doesn't even remember. But she did. I was there. We all saw it."

— a fourteen-year-old girl describing the drugging and sexual assault of her girlfriend at a party

medical use and high abuse potential. The authorizing bill was named after Samantha Reid, the girl in the Michigan case cited above, and seventeen-year-old Hillory J. Farias of Texas, who died in 1996 after ingesting a soft drink containing GHB.[15]

Prescription GHB

It remains to be seen how the recent FDA approval of GHB by prescription (called Xyrem), used in the treatment of sleep disorders, will affect the already well-established, widespread abuse of the drug.

"I was at a bar with my girlfriend. We left our drinks on the bar and went to the ladies room. About twenty minutes later it's like I was totally wiped out and could barely stay upright or awake. My whole body was falling down heavy. I was lucky. My friend was okay, stayed with me, and took me home. I didn't wake up until the afternoon of the next day. I didn't feel normal until twenty-four hours after that. Anything could have happened to me and I would have had no idea what."

— a young woman unknowingly drugged
in a bar, possibly with Rohypnol

15. Tobacco

Observable Indications of Use	Bad breath Smell of tobacco Shortness of breath Nagging cough Discolored teeth
Effects of Use	Increased attention Stress and anxiety reduction Nausea Dizziness
Duration of Effects	30 minutes
Signs of Overdose	Nausea, vomiting Weakness, dizziness Pallor Headache
Fatal Overdose Possible	Yes, from poisoning due to accidental ingestion of or skin contact with nicotine containing insecticides, or consumption of tobacco or tobacco juice **IMPORTANT: If you suspect a person may have overdosed on tobacco, call 911 and seek emergency medical treatment immediately.**

A cigarette is made of dried leaves of the tobacco plant that are rolled up inside thin paper; the user ignites the cigarette to inhale the smoke. In all fifty states it is illegal for people under the age of eighteen to purchase cigarettes. The penalties and the extent to which the law is enforced vary considerably from town to town and state to state.

Bidis (pronounced "beadies") are a type of cigarette imported from Asia. They are small, brown cigarettes, sometimes flavored in vanilla or chocolate, that are hand-rolled tobacco in a leaf with a string at the end. The nicotine content is up to seven times greater than in American cigarettes. They also contain three times more carbon monoxide and five times more tar. They are growing in popularity among young people and often lack the warning label of the surgeon general.[1] Other "herbal cigarettes" are sometimes advertised in popular pro–drug abuse periodicals.

The primary addictive component in tobacco is nicotine. Cigarettes are also known as butts, smokes, spikes, and cigs. A cigarette delivers nicotine to the brain and stimulates the nervous system. Nicotine is readily absorbed through the mucosal linings of the mouth, nose, and lungs and reaches the brain very quickly, within ten seconds. While smokers of cigars and pipes and users of smokeless tobacco do not inhale, the nicotine is absorbed through the mucosal membranes of the mouth.

Effects and Consequences of Use

Nicotine is addictive and acts on the same pleasure centers of the brain as other drugs such as heroin and cocaine do.[2] The behavioral and pharmacologic conditions that define nicotine addiction are similar to those that define addiction to other substances as well.[3] In fact, in some research studies, animals cannot distinguish between the effects of nicotine and cocaine.[4]

The major reason smoking is so rewarding is that it distributes nicotine to the brain very rapidly. Although first-time users of cigarettes may feel dizzy, get a headache, and even vomit, more experienced users report a reduction in tension and fatigue and a boost in concentration. These effects fade in several minutes, but because they were so rewarding, the user wants to repeat the experience.

A cigarette delivers nicotine to the brain with every single puff, with about ten puffs per cigarette over a five-minute period. The actual amount of nicotine delivered in smoke ranges from 0.5 to 2 milligrams per cigarette. A person smoking a pack of cigarettes per day gets two hundred hits of nicotine and learns to regulate his or her mood state by timing the delivery of nicotine to either increase attention or reduce anxiety.[5]

Tolerance to nicotine quickly develops, and users soon need more to achieve the desired effect. This tolerance, in turn, leads to increased dependence and addiction.

Most smokers rapidly progress to regular use and eventual dependence on cigarettes. Smokers continue to smoke more not only to achieve the desired effects as tolerance develops but also to avoid the undesirable effects of withdrawal.

Nicotine withdrawal occurs within a few hours of the last cigarette. During this time the user experiences craving, irritability, cognitive and attention deficits, appetite arousal, and sleep disturbances. These symptoms can last for up to a month, but hunger and craving can persist for six months or longer.[6]

———

"Very few consumers are aware of the effects of nicotine, i.e., its addictive nature and that nicotine is a poison."

— 1978 Brown and Williamson memo

Smoking is the leading preventable cause of death in the United States, killing roughly 430,000 people annually.[7] Tobacco use causes one of every five deaths in the United States. The health consequences of tobacco use are the function of the duration and frequency of use.

Scientists have identified more than forty chemicals in tobacco smoke that cause cancer in humans and animals. Smoking can cause cancer of the lung, larynx, esophagus, mouth, and bladder in addition to chronic lung disease (emphysema and chronic bronchitis), coronary heart disease, and stroke. Smoking also contributes to cancer of the pancreas, cervix, and kidney. Smokeless tobacco and cigars increase the risk of oral cancer and cancer of the lung, larynx, and esophagus. Smoking accounts for one-third of all cancers and about 90% of lung cancer cases. The overall death rates from cancer are twice as high among smokers compared with nonsmokers.[8]

Environmental tobacco smoke (ETS) is smoke that is not intentionally inhaled. It is also known as passive, second-hand, or involuntary smoking. Exposure to ETS increases the risk of cancer and heart disease and exacerbates other respiratory conditions such as asthma. The Environmental Protection Agency estimates that exposure to ETS causes 3,000 nonsmoking Americans to die of lung cancer annually, which is 3% of the annual lung cancer toll. Nonsmokers who are married to heavy smokers have a two to three times greater risk of developing lung cancer, compared with those married to nonsmokers. Exposure to ETS also increases the risk of coronary heart disease.[9]

Children of smokers grow up with exposure to ETS. Roughly 300,000 children annually suffer from lower respiratory tract infections due to ETS. Children raised in smoking homes are more prone to colds, bronchitis, pneumonia, ear infections, reduced lung function, and allergies than children living in smoke-free environments. Careless handling of lit cigarettes is the leading cause of residential fires in the United States, which result in 1,000 deaths annually.[10]

The earlier the age of onset of tobacco use, the more likely one is to develop long-term nicotine addiction and the more likely one is to be a heavy user. Smoking in adolescence affects the rate of lung growth and compromises lung function. Most teen smokers say they would like to quit, but they are difficult to recruit and retain in formal smoking cessation programs. An estimated five million children alive today in the United States will die prematurely due to smoking.[11]

The economic toll of tobacco use in the United States is enormous: at least $50 billion annually in health care costs and another $50 billion in indirect costs.[12]

Primary User Groups

About 55.7 million people in the United States were current cigarette smokers in 2000 (24.9% of the population age twelve and older). The smoking rate was highest among people age eighteen to twenty-five years (38.3%) and lowest among people age twelve to seventeen (13.4%). Of youth age twelve to seventeen who smoke, 46% reported that they personally bought cigarettes in the past month, even though laws in all fifty states prohibit sales to youth under age eighteen.[13]

Smokeless tobacco use was reported by 3.4% of the population. Among people age eighteen to twenty-five, the rate was highest (5.0%) and among people age twelve to seventeen the lowest (2.1%).

Cigar smoking was reported by 4.8% of the population. People age eighteen to twenty-five reported the highest rate (10.4%), and people age twelve to seventeen reported the lowest rate (4.5%).

Most people start smoking as adolescents. An estimated 1.7 million youth between the ages of twelve and seventeen began smoking in 1998. The average age of first tobacco use was 15.4 years.[14]

> "Do we really want to tout cigarette smoke
> as a drug? It is, of course."
>
> — 1969 memo from a Philip Morris researcher

More than half of all students in tenth and twelfth grades have tried cigarettes at least once. Current cigarette use was reported by 12.2% of eighth graders, 21.3% of tenth graders, and 29.5% of high school seniors. Almost one out of every five high school seniors (19.0%) smokes cigarettes every day. Daily cigarette use was also reported by 5.5% of eighth graders and 12.2% of tenth graders. Seven percent of seniors used bidis in the past year.[15]

Teenagers who smoke, compared with those who don't, report higher levels of fighting, attempted suicide, carrying weapons, higher-risk sexual behavior, and alcohol

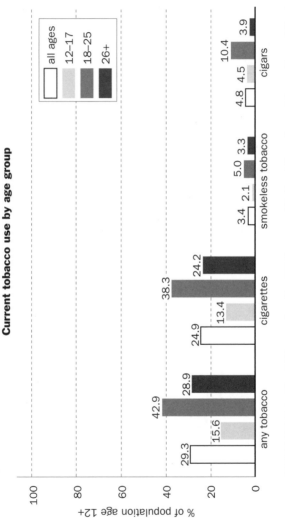

Figure 29

Current tobacco use by age group

Legend:
- all ages
- 12–17
- 18–25
- 26+

any tobacco
- 29.3
- 15.6
- 42.9
- 28.9

cigarettes
- 24.9
- 13.4
- 38.3
- 24.2

smokeless tobacco
- 3.4
- 2.1
- 5.0
- 3.3

cigars
- 4.8
- 4.5
- 10.4
- 3.9

% of population age 12+

SOURCE: 2000 *National Household Survey on Drug Abuse*, U.S. Department of Health and Human Services, Substance Abuse and Mental Health Services Administration, Office of Applied Studies, 2001. CURRENT USE=any use in past month.

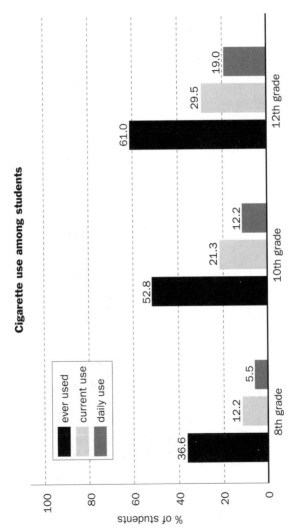

Figure 30

Cigarette use among students

% of students

- ever used
- current use
- daily use

8th grade
- 36.6
- 12.2
- 5.5

10th grade
- 52.8
- 21.3
- 12.2

12th grade
- 61.0
- 29.5
- 19.0

SOURCE: *2001 Monitoring the Future Study*, Institute for Social Research, University of Michigan. EVER USED=use at least once in lifetime. CURRENT USE=any use in past month. DAILY USE=use every day in past thirty days.

229

Figure 31

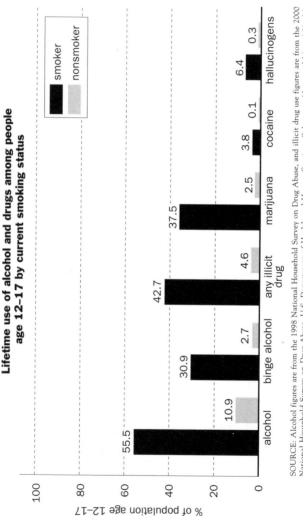

Lifetime use of alcohol and drugs among people age 12-17 by current smoking status

SOURCE: Alcohol figures are from the 1998 National Household Survey on Drug Abuse, and illicit drug use figures are from the 2000 National Household Survey on Drug Abuse, U.S. Department of Health and Human Services, Substance Abuse and Mental Health Services Administration, Office of Applied Studies, 2001. SMOKER=any cigarette use in the past month. LIFETIME USE=use at least once in lifetime.

and other drug use. Cigarette smoking itself does not cause these other high-risk behaviors among youth, but cigarettes are typically the first substance used in a progression that can eventually include alcohol, marijuana, and other drugs. Youth age twelve to seventeen who smoked are much more likely to drink heavily and use illicit drugs than those who didn't smoke.[16]

Delaying the onset of tobacco use may help avert or prevent the likelihood of other high-risk behaviors as well. For this reason, drug and alcohol abuse prevention programs targeting youth are well advised to also address tobacco.

The association between smoking and the use of alcohol and other drugs carries over into adulthood as well. Among past month smokers in 2000, 39.4% were binge alcohol users, 13.6% were heavy alcohol users, and 15.6% were current illicit drug users. Among nonsmokers 14.4% were binge alcohol users, 3.0% were heavy alcohol users and 3.2% were current illicit drug users.[17]

Use of Alcohol and Drugs in Total Population (Age Twelve and Older) by Smoking Status

	SMOKERS	NONSMOKERS
Binge alcohol	39.4%	14.4%
Heavy alcohol	13.6%	3.0%
Illicit drug use	15.6%	3.2%

SOURCE: *2000 National Household Survey on Drug Abuse*, U.S. Department of Health and Human Services, Substance Abuse and Mental Health Services Administration, 2001.

Recent Developments

Little was known about the health effects of smoking when the twentieth century began. One hundred years later, more than fifty-five million Americans still smoke although the health risks of smoking are well established.

Smoking Is Harmful to Health: A Century of Science

A long series of scientific and health community inquiries resulted in public reports and policy interventions that helped change the way we view smoking today. The growth of the antismoking movement led to the 1998 Master Settlement Agreement between the large tobacco companies and the attorneys general of forty-six states.[18]

Ever since the first report that linked cigarette smoking with cancer—the 1964 report of the surgeon general—the tobacco reform movement in the United States has gained momentum. Subsequent reports on smoking and health by the surgeon general, secret industry research documents uncovered in litigation, and formal inquiries by the U.S. FDA have furthered our understanding not only of nicotine addiction and the health hazards of smoking but also of decades-long tobacco industry efforts to deny these claims.[19]

Lawsuits against the Tobacco Industry and the Master Settlement Agreement

Perhaps the most significant events in recent history are the state lawsuits filed against the tobacco industry, the Master Settlement Agreement, and the proposed regulation of tobacco by the FDA. Some of the lawsuits against the tobacco industry filed by states used product-liability approaches to challenge the tobacco companies on the grounds that their products are harmful. The Minnesota lawsuit, and many of those that followed, charged the industry for violations of state antitrust and consumer fraud laws. All suits sought to recover damages for the costs incurred by states in treating sick smokers. Eventually more than forty states filed lawsuits, most of them alleging that the industry violated antitrust laws, engaged in consumer fraud, conspired to withhold information about the health effects of smoking and to withhold low-risk products from the market, concealed damaging research from the public, marketed products to children, or manipulated nicotine levels to keep smokers addicted.

Four states—Mississippi, Florida, Texas, and Minnesota—settled their lawsuits with the tobacco industry by early 1998. Each state was awarded several billion dollars, and the conditions of each settlement varied by state. In late 1998 the attorneys general of the remaining forty-six states announced a historic settlement with the tobacco industry. The $206 billion settlement was the largest financial recovery in U.S. history.

The tobacco industry agreed to restrict advertising (no billboards, no advertising to children), to establish national public education and research funds, to create a foundation to curb teen smoking, and to dissolve the tobacco industry's lobbying arm. In exchange, the agreement settled all pending and future claims by states for Medicaid reimbursement and civil claims based on industry action taken before the settlement. It also granted the industry protection against all future state claims based on exposure to the products.

"Smoking a cigarette for a beginner is a symbolic act . . . 'I am no longer my mother's child, I am tough, I am an adventurer, I'm not square.'. . . As the force from the psychological symbolism subsides, the pharmacological effect takes over to sustain the habit. . . ."

— 1969 draft memo to the
Philip Morris Board of Directors

In the course of Minnesota's lawsuit, the tobacco industry was forced to turn over millions of previously secret tobacco industry documents. These documents, most of which are now open to the public, revealed that the industry knew for thirty years that tobacco is a drug and that nicotine is addictive. The documents also revealed that companies controlled nicotine levels, used ammonia and other compounds to boost nicotine's impact, and marketed their products to young smokers.

These documents, with the incriminating information they contain, have given new life to private litigation against the industry in the form of individual lawsuits by injured smokers and class action suits on behalf of large groups of victims. Many of these lawsuits have been decided against the tobacco industry.

Tobacco Regulation by the FDA?

The battle to grant regulatory control of tobacco to the FDA remains ongoing.

And as this battle for regulation continues, the way America views tobacco will undergo radical change in the twenty-first century. We will witness public education campaigns and changes in public policy that have only just begun in some parts of the country.[20] Smoke-free bars and restaurants will become more commonplace, and resources to help addicted smokers more available.

Nicotine does not impair judgment to the extent of many other drugs. People driving under the influence of nicotine, for example, are not as likely to have car crashes as people driving under the influence of other drugs or alcohol. Yet while smoking does not threaten the public *safety* to the same degree as other drugs, it is clearly *the* primary preventable threat to the public health.

16. Other Substances of Abuse

Many substances are intentionally consumed primarily for their mood-altering effects.

Caffeine

Caffeine consumption in the United States is widespread. The primary sources of caffeine are coffee, tea, carbonated beverages, chocolates, dietary supplements, and some drugs. An estimated 80% of American adults consume coffee on a daily basis. Average daily consumption is 200 mg, the equivalent of about two cups of coffee.[1] A growing number of beverages marketed as energy drinks contain high concentrations of caffeine. Some are even used as mixers with alcohol to allegedly produce "a better high" or reduce hangovers.

Caffeine is a stimulant that increases alertness, reduces fatigue, increases respiration, disrupts sleep, and reduces cerebral blood flow. Fatal caffeine overdoses are possible, and dependence is common. Withdrawal symptoms occur eighteen hours after the last dose of caffeine: headache, fatigue, anxiety, impaired motor performance, nausea, and craving.[2] Numerous studies have examined the role of coffee and caffeine intake as risk factors in peptic ulcer disease, cardiovascular disease, benign breast disease, and pancreatic cancer, with inconsistent, mixed findings.[3]

Dietary/Nutritional Supplements

The Dietary Supplement Health and Education Act of 1994 defines a *dietary supplement* as a product taken by mouth that contains an ingredient designed to supplement the diet. Dietary supplements include minerals, herbs, vitamins, metabolites, glandulars, organ tissues, enzymes, amino acids, concentrates, extracts, and botanicals.[4]

Some dietary supplements are used as mood-enhancing substances of abuse and taken solely to induce an intoxicated state.[5] Some are even marketed with names that mimic illegal drugs with similar effects, such as Ecstasy and methamphetamine tablets. Others, such as GBL-containing nutritional supplements (see page 215), are marketed as sleep aids, muscle-stimulating growth hormones, or aphrodisiacs.

Prescription and over-the-counter (OTC) nonprescription drugs undergo a rigorous approval process administered by the U.S. Food and Drug Administration (FDA), which assures American consumers that these drugs are safe, effective, and marketed in a manner that does not overstate the effects. The FDA monitors and reviews the biomedical development and clinical trials of drugs under development, and the pharmaceutical company must demonstrate both safety and effectiveness prior to FDA approval. Panels of experts review the scientific evidence, and if the health benefit of a drug outweighs the risk, the FDA approves its use for human consumption.

The FDA monitors the frequency of unexpected and adverse reactions, reviews the evidence about drug interactions and appropriate dosages, and sets standards for drug quality and manufacturing. The FDA reviews, approves, and requires product and package insert labeling for both consumer and medical audiences. Advertising of prescription drugs is regulated by the FDA, and advertising of OTC drugs is regulated by the Federal Trade Commission.

With dietary supplements, however, the manufacturer is responsible for ensuring safety prior to marketing and there are no provisions for FDA approval (for safety and effectiveness) before marketing.[6] As a result, dietary supplements lack uniformity in terms of strength, recommended dosages, quality, and manufacture. Health claims are often vague, nonspecific, and potentially lacking in scientific support.[7]

The following list, derived from FDA sources, demonstrates the types of dangers inherent in the use of some of these substances.[8]

Herbal ingredient: chaparral (a traditional American Indian medicine)

Possible health hazards: liver disease, possibly irreversible

Herbal ingredient: comfrey

Possible health hazards: obstruction of blood flow, possibly leading to death

Herbal ingredient: ephedra (also known as ma huang, Chinese ephedra, and epitonin)

Possible health hazards: ranges from high blood pressure, irregular heartbeat, nerve damage, injury, insomnia, tremors, and headaches to seizures, heart attack, stroke, and death

Herbal ingredient: germander

Possible health hazards: liver disease, possibly leading to death

Herbal ingredient: kava

Possible health hazards: liver-related injuries, hepatitis, cirrhosis, and liver failure

Herbal ingredient: lobelia (also known as Indian tobacco)

Possible health hazards: range from breathing problems at low doses to sweating, rapid heartbeat, low blood pressure, and possibly coma or death at higher doses

Herbal ingredient: magnolia-stephania preparation

Possible health hazards: kidney disease, possibly leading to permanent kidney failure

Herbal ingredient: willow bark

Possible health hazards: Reye's syndrome, a potentially fatal disease associated with aspirin intake in children with chicken pox or flu symptoms; allergic reaction in adults. (Willow bark is marketed as an aspirin-free product, although it actually contains an ingredient that converts to the same active ingredient in aspirin.)

Herbal ingredient: wormwood

Possible health hazards: neurological symptoms, characterized by numbness of legs and arms, loss of intellect, delirium, and paralysis

Ephedrine-Based Supplements

Because dietary supplements are largely unregulated, a growing number of products are marketed to young people seeking intoxicating and euphoric effects.

In 1996 the FDA issued a warning to consumers about the dangers of over-the-counter products containing the botanical *ephedrine*, which were marketed as "natural alternatives" to the street drug MDMA or Ecstasy (see page 191), a methamphetamine with hallucinogenic properties. The warning was issued in response to numerous reports of serious illnesses, injuries, and deaths associated with the use of ephedrine-containing dietary supplements. Possible adverse effects include heart attack, stroke, seizures, psychosis, and death, as well as less significant effects such as dizziness, headache, gastrointestinal distress, irregular heartbeat, and heart palpitations. By 1994 the FDA had documented more than eight hundred adverse reactions and fifteen possible deaths from ephedrine-containing supplements.[9]

Many products that contain ephedrine are advertised as sports medicines or legal drug alternatives on the Internet under various brand names. There are even "herbal" cigarettes that do not contain tobacco. They are packaged in ways that appeal to adolescents and others with "active lifestyles." For example, some are called energy boosters or blasters. The packaging indicates that they are stimulating products of 100% natural herbs or botanicals that can make the user feel great, all day long. The instructions concerning dosage are equally vague, such as "Take more to achieve a greater effect." These "pep pills" are often sold at convenience stores, truck stops, gas stations, health food stores, pharmacies, and grocery stores.

Some over-the-counter ephedrine-based products claim to increase energy; heighten physical, mental, and sexual awareness; and sometimes even produce euphoria. Some athletes use these products to enhance physical performance. In a recent study by the National Collegiate Athletic Association, almost 60% of the 21,000 athletes surveyed reported use of unregulated nutritional supplements.[10] In another study of 511 gym patrons, 25% reported ephedrine use.[11]

The ingredients listed in ephedrine-based products may include ma huang, ma huang extract, Chinese ephedra, ephedra sinica, ephedra extract, ephedra herb powder, epitonin, or ephedrine, any of which indicate the presence of ephedrine. Many so-called energy drinks also contain ephedra, which when combined with caffeine are particularly dangerous.

In 1997 the FDA proposed rules on labeling and marketing and in April 2000 issued guidance for industry about "street drug alternatives" in light of their high potential for abuse, threat to public health, and increasing abuse by young people.[12] The FDA stated that these products will be considered unapproved and misbranded drugs that are subject to regulatory action, including seizure.[13]

Ephedrine is also the active ingredient in many over-the-counter allergy medications and the primary chemical used in the illicit manufacture of methamphetamine. To contain its use in methamphetamine manufacture, some stores have limited the amounts that can be purchased by a single customer. In 2001 Health Canada issued a voluntary recall of ephedrine and ephedra products in Canada, citing a "serious health risk" posed by ingesting large amounts.

Dextromethorphan (DXM, DM, Robo)

Isolated reports have surfaced over the past fifteen years about adolescents abusing over-the-counter cough products that contain dextromethorphan, a cough suppressant. Isolated cases of overdose and death have occurred. Some abusers report drinking up to four eight-ounce bottles per day. Dextramethorphan is also the active ingredient in some over-the-counter cold preparations in pill form.

Recipes have also surfaced on how to extract the active dextromethorphan and convert it into a white powder. The powder is then snorted, put into capsules, or pressed into pills. Some Internet sites give detailed dosage instructions based on the user's body weight and other characteristics. These pills sell for about five dollars each. Dextromethorphan has also been sold as Ecstasy and been identified as a cut in heroin, illicit street drugs, and other drugs.[14]

People intoxicated on dextromethorphan may refer to themselves as "robo cops" or call the experience "robo tripping" due to hallucinations and altered time perception. Others refer to it as "sipping syrup" when they consume cough syrup with dextramethorphan or prescription cough syrup containing codeine. Some call the groggy feeling "drippy" and talk of reaching various "zones" and "plateaus." Some users describe feeling numb all over, which enables them to slam dance or intentionally crash into and bounce off objects such as walls without pain.

Other effects include slurred speech, sweating, uncoordinated movements, and high blood pressure.[15]

Steroids

Anabolic steroids are synthetic compounds similar to male sex hormones (androgens). They are medically prescribed to correct testosterone imbalances related to delayed onset of puberty or impotence and are used in the treatment of body wasting (loss of lean muscle mass) due to diseases such as AIDS.

Unlike the other drugs of abuse discussed in this book, steroids are *not* taken primarily for their psychoactive, mood-altering effects. People take steroids illegally to enhance physical performance or improve physical appearance by boosting muscle growth. They are diverted from pharmacies, smuggled in from other countries, or illicitly made in labs. In addition, steroidal dietary supplements (such as androsterone—DHEA—and androstenedione—Andro) can be purchased legally at health food stores and gyms.

Steroids are taken orally, rubbed on as a gel or lotion, or are injected intramuscularly. They are typically used over a period of weeks or months, followed by a period of abstinence, which is then followed by another period of use. This is known as "cycling," or "pyramiding." Using different types of steroids to minimize negative effects is known as "stacking."[16]

Adverse physical side effects from steroid use include increased risk of liver tumors and cancer, kidney tumors and cancer, heart attack, and fluid retention, hypertension, jaundice, severe acne, hair loss, and trembling. Men experience shrinking testicles, development of breasts, lowered sperm count, and increased risk of prostate cancer. Women experience masculinization, including growth of facial hair, coarsened skin, deepened voice, and loss of menstrual cycle. Adolescents risk being short in stature for the remainder of their lives if they take steroids before their adolescent growth spurt. Some of these effects subside with discontinuation of use, while others are irreversible.[17]

Negative psychological side effects include aggression, temper outbursts ("roid rage"), manic symptoms, insomnia, nervous irritability, and delusions. Many users report feeling invincible and good while using steroids. While withdrawing from use, depression is common and can last up to a year after cessation of use.

How many people abuse steroids? An estimated 1.5 million gymnasium clients in the United States may have used adrenal hormones.[18] According to the 2000 Monitoring the Future Study, past year use of steroids was reported by 2.2% of eighth-grade boys, 2.8% of tenth-grade boys, and 2.5% of high school senior boys.[19]

Notes

Chapter 1:
Overview of Drug and Alcohol Abuse
in the United States

1. U.S. Department of Health and Human Services, Substance Abuse and Mental Health Services Administration, Office of Applied Studies, *Summary of Findings from the 2000 National Household Survey on Drug Abuse*, NHSDA Series: H–13 (Rockville, Md.: DHHS, 2001). DHHS publication no. (SMA) 01–3549.

2. U.S. Department of Health and Human Services, Substance Abuse and Mental Health Services Administration, Office of Applied Studies, *Worker Drug Use and Workplace Policies and Programs: Results from the 1994 and 1997 National Household Survey on Drug Abuse* (Rockville, Md.: DHHS, 1999). DHHS publication no. (SMA) 99–3352.

3. Tobacco-related deaths are from the U.S. Department of Health and Human Services, Centers for Disease Control and Prevention, "Achievements in Public Health, 1900–1999: Tobacco Use—United States, 1900–1999," *Morbidity and Mortality Weekly Report* vol. 48, no. 43 (1999). Alcohol-related causes are from the National Institutes of Health, National Institute on Alcohol Abuse and Alcoholism, "State Trends in Alcohol Problems, 1979–92," *U.S. Alcohol Epidemiologic Data Reference Manual* vol. 5, first edition (September 1996). NIH publication no. 96–4174. Traffic fatalities are from H. Yi, F. S. Stinson, G. D. Williams, and D. Bertolucci, National Institute on Alcohol Abuse and Alcoholism, Division of Biometry and Epidemiology, Alcohol Epidemiologic Data System, "Trends in Alcohol-Related Fatal Traffic Crashes, United States, 1975–1997," *Surveillance Report* no. 49 (December 1999). Drug-induced deaths include those due to drug use and abuse and poisoning from medically prescribed drugs, and it

247

excludes accidents, homicides, and other causes directly related and newborn deaths where maternal drug use during pregnancy was a significant contributing condition. Drug-induced deaths and deaths from suicide, AIDS, and homicide are from the U.S. Department of Health and Human Services, Centers for Disease Control and Prevention, National Center for Health Statistics, "Deaths: Final Data for 1997," *National Vital Statistics Reports* vol. 47, no. 19 (30 June 1999).

4. U.S. Department of Health and Human Services, Substance Abuse and Mental Health Services Administration, Office of Applied Studies, *National Household Survey on Drug Abuse: Population Estimates 1998* (Rockville, Md.: DHHS, 1999). DHHS publication no. (SMA) 99–3327. To assess "dependence," the National Household Survey on Drug Abuse included a series of questions based on *The Diagnostic and Statistical Manual of Mental Disorders*, 4th ed. (DSM-IV) of the American Psychological Association.

5. U.S. Department of Health and Human Services, Public Health Service, Centers for Disease Control and Prevention, National Center for HIV, STD, and TB Prevention, *HIV/AIDS Surveillance Report: U.S. HIV and AIDS Surveillance Report 2001* vol. 13, no. 1 (2001).

6. U.S. Department of Health and Human Services, Department of Health and Human Services, Centers for Disease Control and Prevention, *If You Have Hepatitis C* (Rockville, Md.: DHHS, 1998).

7. U.S. Centers for Disease Control and Prevention, *Hepatitis C Epidemiology: Transmission Modes*. Available on-line at www.cdc.gov.

8. U.S. Department of Health and Human Services, National Institutes of Health, National Institute on Drug Abuse, "Infectious Disease and Drug Abuse," *NIDA Notes* vol. 14, no. 2 (1999).

9. National Center on Addiction and Substance Abuse, *Dangerous Liaisons: Substance Abuse and Sex* (New York: Columbia University, 1999). Available on-line at www.casacolumbia.org/publications1456/publications.htm.

10. U.S. Department of Health and Human Services, Inspector General, *Youth and Alcohol: Dangerous and Deadly Consequences: Report to the Surgeon General* (Rockville, Md.: DHHS, 1992), as summarized in National Clearinghouse for Alcohol and Drug Information, "Sex Under the Influence of Alcohol and Other Drugs," *Making the Link Fact Sheets* (1995). NCADI inventory no. ML005.

11. American Academy of Pediatrics, Committee on Adolescence, "Sexually Transmitted Diseases," *Pediatrics* vol. 94, no. 4 (1994).

12. U.S. Department of Health and Human Services, Public Health Service, Centers for Disease Control and Prevention, "Trends in Sexual Risk Behaviors Among High School Students— United States 1991–1997," *Morbidity and Mortality Weekly Report* vol. 47, no. 36 (1998).

13. U.S. Department of Health and Human Services, National Institutes of Health, National Institute on Drug Abuse, "Infectious Disease and Drug Abuse," *NIDA Notes* vol. 14, no. 2 (1999).

14. U.S. Department of Health and Human Services, National Institutes of Health, National Institute on Drug Abuse, *National Pregnancy and Health Survey—Drug Use Among Women Delivering Livebirths: 1992* (Rockville, Md.: DHHS, 1996). NIH publication no. 96–3819.

15. U.S. Department of Health and Human Services, National Institutes of Health, National Institute on Drug Abuse, *Nicotine Addiction* (Rockville, Md.: DHHS, 1998). NIH publication no. 98–4342.

16. U.S. Department of Health and Human Services, National Institutes of Health, National Institute on Alcohol Abuse and Alcoholism, "Fetal Alcohol Syndrome," *Alcohol Alert* no. 13, PH 297 (1991).

17. J. L. Jacobson and S. W. Jacobson, "Drinking Moderately and Pregnancy: Effects on Child Development," *Alcohol Research and Health* vol. 23, no. 1 (1999).

18. U.S. Department of Health and Human Services, National Institutes of Health, National Institute on Alcohol Abuse and Alcoholism, *Alcohol: What You Don't Know Can Harm You* (Rockville, Md.: DHHS, 1999). NIH publication no. 99–4323.

19. U.S. Department of Health and Human Services, National Institutes of Health, National Institute on Drug Abuse, "Prenatal Exposure to Drugs of Abuse May Affect Later Behavior and Learning," *NIDA Notes* vol. 13, no. 4 (1998).

20. National Center on Addiction and Substance Abuse, *The Costs of Substance Abuse to America's Health Care System, Report 1: Medicaid Hospital Costs* (New York: Columbia University, 1993), as summarized in National Clearinghouse for Alcohol and Drug Information, "Health Care Costs, the Deficit and Alcohol, Tobacco, and Other Drugs," *Making the Link Series* (Spring 1995). NCADI inventory no. ML007.

21. U.S. Department of Health and Human Services, Substance Abuse and Mental Health Services Administration, Office of Applied Studies, *Emergency Department Trends from the Drug Abuse Warning Network, Preliminary Estimates January–June 2001 with Revised Estimates 1994 to 2000,* DAWN Series: D–20 (Rockville, Md.: DHHS, 2002). DHHS publication no. (SMA) 02–3634.

22. Center for Substance Abuse Research, University of Maryland, College Park, "For First Time in Fifty Years More Than One-Third of U.S. Adults Say Drinking Caused Family Trouble," *CESAR Fax* vol. 8, no. 47 (1999).

23. B. F. Grant, "Estimates of U.S. Children Exposed to Alcohol Abuse and Dependence in the Family," *American Journal of Public Health* vol. 90, no. 1 (2000).

24. U.S. Department of Health and Human Services, National Institutes of Health, National Institute on Alcohol Abuse and Alcoholism, "Children of Alcoholics: Are They Different?" *Alcohol Alert* no. 9, PH 288 (1990).

25. U.S. Department of Health and Human Services, Substance Abuse and Mental Health Services Administration, Office of

Applied Studies, *Worker Drug Use and Workplace Policies and Programs: Results from the 1994 and 1997 National Household Survey on Drug Abuse* (Rockville, Md.: DHHS, 1999). DHHS publication no. (SMA) 99–3352.

26. U.S. Department of Justice, Office of Justice Programs, *Substance Abuse and Treatment, State and Federal Prisoners, 1997*, Special Report (Washington, D.C.: Bureau of Justice Statistics, 1999). NCJ–172871.

27. Ibid.

28. National Clearinghouse on Alcohol and Drug Information, "Violence and Crime and Alcohol and Other Drugs," *Making the Link Series* (Spring 1995). NCADI inventory no. ML002.

29. U.S. Department of Health and Human Services, National Institutes of Health, National Institute on Alcohol Abuse and Alcoholism, "Alcohol, Violence and Aggression," *Alcohol Alert* no. 38 (1997).

30. U.S. Department of Justice, Office of Justice Programs, National Institute of Justice, *ADAM Preliminary 2000 Findings on Drug Use and Drug Markets–Adult Male Arrestees* (Washington, D.C.: Department of Justice, 2001). NIJ–189101.

31. Office of National Drug Control Policy, *The Economic Costs of Drug Abuse in the United States, 1992–1998* (Washington, D.C.: Executive Office of the President, 2001). NCJ–190636.

32. Office of National Drug Control Policy, Office of Programs, Budget, Research and Evaluation, *What America's Users Spend on Illegal Drugs: 1988–2000* (Cambridge, Mass.: Office of National Drug Control Policy, 2001). NCJ–192334, PO no. 3264.

33. U.S. Department of Justice, National Drug Intelligence Center, *Drugs and the Internet: An Overview of the Threat to America's Youth* (Johnstown, Penn.: Department of Justice, 2001), p. 3.

34. E. Drucker, "Harm Reduction: A Public Health Strategy," *Current Issues in Public Health 1* (1995): 64–70. Available on-line at www.lindesmith.org/library/tlcdruck.html (accessed 28 February 2000).

35. U.S. Department of Health and Human Services, Centers for Disease Control and Prevention, "Update: Syringe Exchange Programs—United States, 1997," *Morbidity and Mortality Weekly Report* vol. 47, no. 31 (1998).

36. R. L. DuPont and E. A. Voth, "Drug Legalization, Harm Reduction, and Drug Policy," *Annals of Internal Medicine* vol. 123, no. 6 (1995).

37. U.S. Department of Health and Human Services, Substance Abuse and Mental Health Services Administration, Office of Applied Studies, *Treatment Episode Data Set (TEDS) 1994–1999, National Admissions to Substance Abuse Treatment Services*, DASIS Series: S–14 (Rockville, Md.: DHHS, 2001). DHHS publication no. (SMA) 01–3550.

38. U.S. Department of Health and Human Services, National Institutes of Health, National Institute on Drug Abuse, *Principles of Drug Addiction Treatment: A Research-Based Guide* (Rockville, Md.: DHHS, 1999). NIH publication no. 99–4180.

39. D. R. Gerstein, R. A. Johnson, H. Harwood, D. Fountain, N. Suter, and K. Malley, *Evaluating Recovery Services: The California Drug and Alcohol Treatment Assessment (CALDATA)*, California Department of Alcohol and Drug Programs (Chicago: National Opinion Research Center, 1994). Executive summary available on-line at www.adp.cahwnet.gov/pdf/caldata.pdf (accessed 13 May 2000).

40. Join Together, *Treatment for Addiction: Advancing the Common Good—Recommendations from a Join Together Policy Panel on Treatment and Recovery* (Boston: Boston University School of Public Health, 1998). Available on-line at www.jointogether.org/sa/.

41. Ibid.

42. B. F. Grant and D. A. Dawson, "Age at Onset of Alcohol Use and Its Association with DSM-IV Alcohol Abuse and Dependence: Results of the National Longitudinal Alcohol Epidemiologic Survey," *Journal of Substance Abuse* vol. 9 (1997): 103–10; J. D. Hawkins, J. W. Graham, E. Maguin, K. G. Hill, and R. F. Catalano,

"Exploring the Effects of Age of Alcohol Use Initiation and Psychosocial Risk Factors on Subsequent Alcohol Misuse," *Journal of Studies on Alcohol* vol. 58 (1997); B. F. Grant and D. A. Dawson, "Age at Onset of Drug Use and Its Association with DSM-IV Drug Abuse and Dependence: Results of the National Longitudinal Alcohol Epidemiologic Survey," *Journal of Substance Abuse* vol. 10 (1998): 163–73.

43. National Center on Addiction and Substance Abuse, *The 1996 National Survey of American Attitudes on Substance Abuse II: Teens and Their Parents* (New York: Columbia University, 1996). Conducted by Luntz Research Companies.

44. D. R. Lyman, R. Milich, R. Zimmerman, S. P. Novak, T. K. Logan, C. Martin, C. Leukefeld, and R. Clayton, "Project DARE: No Effects at 10-Year Follow-Up," *Journal of Consulting and Clinical Psychology* vol. 67, no. 4 (1999); S. T. Ennett, N. S. Tobler, C. L. Ringwalt, and R. L. Flewelling, "How Effective Is Drug Abuse Resistance Education? A Meta-Analysis of Project DARE Outcome Evaluations," *American Journal of Public Health* vol. 84, no. 9 (1994).

45. U.S. Department of Health and Human Services, National Institutes of Health, National Institute on Drug Abuse, *Preventing Drug Use Among Children and Adolescents: A Research-Based Guide* (Rockville, Md.: DHHS, 1997). NIH publication no. 97–4212; C. Perry et al., "Project Northland: Outcomes of a Community-Wide Alcohol Use Prevention Program during Early Adolescence," *American Journal of Public Health* vol. 86, no. 7 (1996).

Chapter 2:
Why Drugs? The Attraction and Harm
of Alcohol and Drug Abuse

1. L. D. Johnston, P. M. O'Malley, and J. G. Bachman, "Drug Trends in 1999 Are Mixed," *1999 Monitoring the Future Study* (Ann Arbor, Mich.: University of Michigan News and Information Services, December 1999). Available on-line at www.monitoringthe future.org (accessed 10 January 2000).

2. U.S. Department of Health and Human Services, National Institutes of Health, National Institute on Drug Abuse, "Protective Factors Can Buffer High-Risk Youth from Drug Use," *NIDA Notes* vol. 11, no. 3 (1996); U.S. Department of Health and Human Services, National Institutes of Health, National Institute on Drug Abuse, *Preventing Drug Use Among Children and Adolescents: A Research-Based Guide* (Rockville, Md.: DHHS, 1997). NIH publication no. 97–4212; J. D. Hawkins, R. F. Catalano, and J. Y. Miller, "Risk and Protective Factors for Alcohol and Other Drug Problems in Adolescence and Early Adulthood: Implications for Substance Abuse Prevention," *Psychological Bulletin* vol. 112, no. 10 (1992): 64–105; M. D. Resnick et al., "Protecting Adolescents from Harm: Findings from the National Longitudinal Study on Adolescent Health," *Journal of the American Medical Association* vol. 278, no. 10 (1997).

3. J. A. Anderson and W. Branigin, "Flood of Contraband Hard to Stop: Mexican Traffickers Benefit from Heavy Traffic, New Technology," *The Washington Post* 2 November 1997, A01.

Chapter 3:
Signs and Symptoms of a Drug or
Alcohol Problem

1. U.S. Department of Health and Human Services, National Institutes of Health, National Institute on Alcohol Abuse and Alcoholism, *Alcohol: Getting the Facts* (Rockville, Md.: DHHS, 1996). NIH publication no. 96–4153.

2. American Psychiatric Association, *Diagnostic and Statistical Manual of Mental Disorders*, 4th ed. (DSM-IV) (Washington, D.C.: APA, 1994), 182.

Chapter 4:
What Is Addiction?

1. U.S. Department of Health and Human Services, National Institutes of Health, National Institute on Alcohol Abuse and Alcoholism, "Alcohol and Trauma," *Alcohol Alert* no. 3 (1989).

2. American Medical Association, Committee on Alcoholism, "Hospitalization of Patients with Alcoholism (Reports of Officers)," *Journal of the American Medical Association* vol. 162 (1956): 750; American Psychiatric Association, *Diagnostic and Statistical Manual of Mental Disorders* (1952); *DSM-II* (1968); *DSM-III* (1978); *DSM-IIIR* (1987); *DSM-IV* (1994) (Washington, D.C.: APA).

3. Physician Leadership on National Drug Policy, *Major New Study Finds Drug Treatment as Good as Treatment for Diabetes, Asthma, Etc., and Better and Cheaper Than Prison*, Press Release (March 1998). Available on-line at www.caas.brown.edu/plndp (accessed 24 April 2000).

4. U.S. Department of Health and Human Services, National Institutes of Health, National Institute on Alcohol Abuse and Alcoholism, *NIAAA Releases New Estimates of Alcohol Abuse and Dependence*, Press Release (March 17, 1995).

5. American Psychiatric Association, *Diagnostic and Statistical Manual of Mental Disorders*, 4th ed. (DSM-IV) (Washington, D.C.: APA, 1994), 181.

6. Ibid., 178.

7. A. I. Leshner, "Addiction Is a Brain Disease and It Matters," *Science* vol. 278, no. 5335 (1997).

Chapter 6:
Important Considerations about Illicit Drug Use

1. U.S. Department of Health and Human Services, National Institutes of Health, National Institute on Drug Abuse, "Rate and Duration of Drug Activity Play Major Roles in Drug Abuse, Addiction, and Treatment," *NIDA Notes* vol. 12, no. 2 (1997).

2. U.S. Department of Health and Human Services, Substance Abuse and Mental Health Services Administration, "Mid-Year 1998 Preliminary Emergency Department Data from the Drug Abuse Warning Network," *Drug Abuse Warning Network Series: D–10* (Rockville, Md.: DHHS, 1999). DHHS publication no. (SMA) 99–3316.

3. C. B. Clayman, ed., *The American Medical Association Guide to Prescription and Over-the-Counter Drugs* (New York: Random House, 1988).

Chapter 7:
Alcohol

1. U.S. Department of Health and Human Services, National Institutes of Health, National Institute on Alcohol Abuse and Alcoholism, *Alcohol: Getting the Facts* (Rockville, Md.: DHHS, 1996). NIH publication no. 96–4153.

2. C. B. Clayman, ed., *The American Medical Association Guide to Prescription and Over-the-Counter Drugs* (New York: Random House, 1988).

3. U.S. Department of Health and Human Services, National Institutes of Health, National Institute on Alcohol Abuse and Alcoholism, *Alcohol Research: Promise for the Decade* (Rockville, Md.: DHHS, 1991). ADM publication no. 92–1990.

4. U.S. Department of Health and Human Services, National Institutes of Health, National Institute on Alcohol Abuse and Alcoholism, "Alcohol and Cancer," *Alcohol Alert* no. 21, PH 345 (1993).

5. U.S. Department of Transportation, National Highway Traffic Safety Administration, *Traffic Safety Facts, 2000* (Washington, D.C.: GPO, 2001). DOT HS 809 323.

6. Ibid.

7. Ibid.

8. Ibid.

9. U.S. Department of Health and Human Services, National Institutes of Health, National Institute on Alcohol Abuse and Alcoholism, *Alcohol: What You Don't Know Can Harm You* (Rockville, Md.: DHHS, 1999). NIH publication no. 99–4323.

10. U.S. Department of Transportation, National Highway Traffic Safety Administration, *Traffic Tech, A Legislative History of .08 Per Se Laws*, no. 256 (2001).

11. R. W. Hingston, T. Heeren, and M. R. Winter, "Preventing Impaired Driving," *Alcohol Research and Health* vol. 23, no. 1 (1999).

12. U.S. Department of Health and Human Services, Substance Abuse and Mental Health Services Administration, Office of Applied Studies, *Summary of Findings from the 2000 National Household Survey on Drug Abuse*, NHSDA Series H–13, (Rockville, Md.: DHHS, 2001). DHHS publication no. (SMA) 01–3549.

13. Ibid.

14. Ibid.

15. Ibid.

16. 2001 Monitoring the Future Study, Institute for Social Research, University of Michigan.

17. Ibid.

18. U.S. Department of Health and Human Services, Substance Abuse and Mental Health Services Administration, Office of Applied Studies, *Treatment Episode Data Set (TEDS) 1994–1999, National Admissions to Substance Abuse Treatment Services*, DASIS Series: S–14 (Rockville, Md.: DHHS, 2001). DHHS publication no. (SMA) 01–3550.

19. B. F. Grant and D. A. Dawson, "Age at Onset of Drug Use and Its Association with DSM-IV Drug Abuse and Dependence: Results of the National Longitudinal Alcohol Epidemiologic Survey," *Journal of Substance Abuse* vol. 10 (1998): 163–73.

20. Ibid.

21. U.S. Department of Health and Human Services, National Institutes of Health, National Institute on Alcohol Abuse and Alcoholism, "College Students and Drinking," *Alcohol Alert* no. 29, PH 357 (July 1995).

Chapter 8:
Cocaine

1. U.S. Department of Health and Human Services, National Institutes of Health, National Institute on Drug Abuse, *NIDA Research Report—Cocaine Abuse and Addiction* (Washington, D.C.: GPO, 1999). NIH publication no. 99–4342.

2. U.S. Department of Health and Human Services, National Institutes of Health, National Institute on Drug Abuse, *Epidemiologic Trends in Drug Abuse; Volume II—Proceedings of the Community Epidemiology Work Group, June 1998* (Washington, D.C.: GPO, 1999). NIH publication no. 99–4301.

3. U.S. Department of Justice, Drug Enforcement Administration, *Drugs of Abuse* (Washington, D.C.: GPO, 1996).

4. *NIDA Research Report—Cocaine Abuse and Addiction.* (See note 1 above.)

5. U.S. Department of Health and Human Services, National Institutes of Health, National Institute on Drug Abuse, "Cocaine Activates Different Brain Regions for Rush Versus Craving," *NIDA Notes* vol. 13, no. 5 (1998).

6. U.S. Department of Health and Human Services, National Institutes of Health, National Institute on Drug Abuse, "Cocaine Abuse May Lead to Strokes and Mental Deficits," *NIDA Notes* vol. 13, no. 3 (1998).

7. *NIDA Research Report—Cocaine Abuse and Addiction*. (See note 1 on page 258.)

8. Ibid.

9. *Drugs of Abuse*. (See note 3 on page 258.)

10. U.S. Department of Health and Human Services, Substance Abuse and Mental Health Services Administration, Office of Applied Studies, *Summary of Findings from the 1998 National Household Survey on Drug Abuse*, NHSDA Series: H–10. (Rockville, Md.: DHHS, 1999). DHHS publication no. (SMA) 99–3328.

11. U.S. Department of Health and Human Services, Substance Abuse and Mental Health Services Administration, Office of Applied Studies, *Summary of Findings from the 2000 National Household Survey on Drug Abuse*, NHSDA Series: H–13 (Rockville, Md.: DHHS, 2001). DHHS publication no. (SMA) 01–3549.

12. Ibid.

13. 2001 Monitoring the Future Study, Institute for Social Research, University of Michigan.

14. U.S. Department of Health and Human Services, Substance Abuse and Mental Health Services Administration, Office of Applied Studies, *Emergency Department Trends from the Drug Abuse Warning Network, Preliminary Estimates January–June 2001 with Revised Estimates 1994 to 2000*, DAWN Series: D–20 (Rockville, Md.: DHHS, 2002). DHHS publication no. (SMA) 02–3634.

15. U.S. Department of Health and Human Services, Substance Abuse and Mental Health Services Administration, Office of Applied Studies, *Treatment Episode Data Set (TEDS) 1994–1999, National Admissions to Substance Abuse Treatment Services*, DASIS Series: S–14 (Rockville, Md.: DHHS, 2001). DHHS publication no. (SMA) 01–3550.

16. Ibid.

17. U.S. Department of Justice, Office of Justice Programs, National Institute of Justice, *1997 Drug Use Forecasting: Annual Report on Drug Use among Adult and Juvenile Arrestees* (Washington, D.C.: GPO, 1998). NCJ–171672.

18. U.S. Department of Justice, Office of Justice Programs, National Institute of Justice, *1998 Annual Report on Drug Use among Adult and Juvenile Arrestees* (Washington, D.C.: GPO, 1999). NCJ–175656.

Chapter 9:
Hallucinogens

1. U.S. Department of Justice, Drug Enforcement Administration, *Drugs of Abuse* (Washington, D.C.: GPO, 1996).

2. Ibid.

3. Ibid.

4. Ibid.; U.S. Department of Justice, Drug Enforcement Administration, "Drugs of Concern," *DEA Briefing Book* (Washington, D.C.: GPO, 1999).

5. American Psychiatric Association, *Diagnostic and Statistical Manual of Mental Disorders*, 4th ed. (DSM-IV) (Washington, D.C.: APA, 1994).

6. Ibid.

7. Ibid.

8. Texas Commission on Alcohol and Drug Abuse, "Fry: A Study of Adolescents' Use of Embalming Fluid with Marijuana and Tobacco," *TCADA Research Brief* (Austin, Tex.: TCADA, 1998).

9. "Drugs of Concern." (See note 4 above.)

10. Ibid.

11. U.S. Department of Health and Human Services, National Institutes of Health, National Institute on Drug Abuse, "PCP (Phencyclidine)," *NIDA Infofax*. Available on-line at www.nida.nih.gov/infofax/pcp.html (accessed 18 February 2000).

12. American Psychiatric Association, *Diagnostic and Statistical Manual of Mental Disorders*. (See note 5 above.)

13. U.S. Department of Health and Human Services, National Institutes of Health, National Institute on Drug Abuse, "Club Drugs," *NIDA Infofax* no. 13674. Available on-line at www.nida.nih.gov/infofax/clubdrugs.html (accessed 18 February 2000).

14. U.S. Department of Justice, Drug Enforcement Administration, Office of Diversion Control, "Ketamine," *Drug and Chemical Evaluation Section* (Washington, D.C.: GPO, 1999). DEA/ODE/991021.

15. "Drugs of Concern." (See note 4 on page 260.)

16. U.S. Department of Health and Human Services, Substance Abuse and Mental Health Services Administration, Office of Applied Studies, *Summary of Findings from the 2000 National Household Survey on Drug Abuse*, NHSDA Series: H–13 (Rockville, Md.: DHHS, 2001). DHHS publication no. (SMA) 01–3549.

17. Ibid.

18. 2001 Monitoring the Future Study, Institute for Social Research, University of Michigan.

19. Ibid.

20. U.S. Department of Health and Human Services, Substance Abuse and Mental Health Services Administration, Office of Applied Studies, *Emergency Department Trends from the Drug Abuse Warning Network, Preliminary Estimates January–June 2001 with Revised Estimates 1994 to 2000*, DAWN Series: D–20 (Rockville, Md.: 2002). DHHS publication no. (SMA) 02–3634.

21. U.S. Department of Health and Human Services, Substance Abuse and Mental Health Services Administration, Office of Applied Studies, *Treatment Episode Data Set (TEDS) 1994–1999, National Admissions to Substance Abuse Treatment Services*, DASIS Series: S–14 (Rockville, Md.: DHHS, 2001). DHHS publication no. (SMA) 01–3550.

22. U.S. Department of Health and Human Services, National Institutes of Health, National Institute on Drug Abuse, *Club Drugs: Community Drug Alert Bulletin* (Rockville, Md.: DHHS, 1999). NIH publication no. 00–4723.

23. A. Milosevic, N. Agrawal, P. Redfearn, and L. Mair, "The Occurrence of Toothwear in Users of Ecstasy (3,4 Methylene-DioxyMethAmphetamine)," *Community Dentistry and Oral Epidemiology* vol. 27 (1999): 283–87.

24. *Club Drugs*. (See note 22 on page 261.)

25. Mark Boal, "Designer Drug Death," *Rolling Stone* (31 January 2002).

26. R. Miller, "We're All Suckers Sometime," *The News-Times* (Danbury, Conn.) 16 July 1995.

27. P. Baker, "Hallucinative Hoax Is Back: LSD Decals Don't Exist," *The Washington Post*, 28 February 1990.

28. J. H. Brunvand, *Curses! Broiled Again!* (New York: Norton, 1989).

Chapter 10:
Heroin/Opiates/Narcotics

1. U.S. Department of Health and Human Services, National Institutes of Health, National Institute on Drug Abuse, "NIH Panel Calls for Expanded Methadone Treatment for Heroin Addiction," *NIDA Notes* vol. 12, no. 6 (1997); U.S. Department of Health and Human Services, National Institutes of Health, National Institute on Drug Abuse, "High Dose Methadone Improves Treatment Outcomes," *NIDA Notes* vol. 14, no. 5 (1999).

2. U.S. Department of Health and Human Services, National Institutes of Health, National Institute on Drug Abuse, *Epidemiologic Trends in Drug Abuse: Volume II—Proceedings of the Community Epidemiology Work Group, June 1998* (Washington, D.C.: GPO, 1999). NIH publication no. 99–4301.

3. U.S. Department of Health and Human Services, National Institutes of Health, National Institute on Drug Abuse, *NIDA Research Report: Heroin Abuse and Addiction* (Rockville, Md.: DHHS, 1997). NIH publication no. 97–4165.

4. U.S. Department of Justice, Drug Enforcement Administration, *Drugs of Abuse* (Washington, D.C.: GPO, 1996).

5. *NIDA Research Report*. (See note 3 above.)

6. U.S. Department of Justice, Drug Enforcement Administration, "Drugs of Concern," *DEA Briefing Book* (Washington, D.C.: GPO, 1999).

7. U.S. Department of Health and Human Services, Substance Abuse and Mental Health Services Administration, Office of Applied Studies, *Summary of Findings from the 2000 National Household Survey on Drug Abuse*, NHSDA Series: H–13 (Rockville, Md.: DHHS, 2001). DHHS publication no. (SMA) 01–3549.

8. Ibid.

9. 2001 Monitoring the Future Study, Institute for Social Research, University of Michigan.

10. U.S. Department of Health and Human Services, Substance Abuse and Mental Health Services Administration, Office of Applied Studies, *Emergency Department Trends from the Drug Abuse Warning Network, Preliminary Estimates January–June 2001 with Revised Estimates 1994 to 2000*, DAWN Series: D–20 (Rockville, Md.: DHHS, 2002). DHHS publication no. (SMA) 02–3634.

11. U.S. Department of Health and Human Services, Substance Abuse and Mental Health Services Administration, Office of Applied Studies, *Treatment Episode Data Set (TEDS) 1994–1999, National Admissions to Substance Abuse Treatment Services*, DASIS Series: S–14 (Rockville, Md.: DHHS, 2001). DHHS publication no. (SMA) 01–3550.

12. Ibid.

13. U.S. Department of Health and Human Services, National Institutes of Health, National Institute on Drug Abuse, "Heroin Update: Smoking, Injecting Cause Similar Effects; Usage Patterns May Be Shifting," *NIDA Notes* vol. 10, no. 4 (1995); U.S. Department of Health and Human Services, National Institutes of Health, National Institute on Drug Abuse, *Epidemiologic Trends in Drug Abuse: Volume II—Proceedings of the Community Epidemiology Work Group, December 1997* (Rockville, Md.: DHHS, 1998). NIH publication no. 98–4298.

14. U.S. Department of Health and Human Services, National Institutes of Health, National Institute on Drug Abuse, "Heroin Snorters Risk Transition to Injection Drug Use and Infectious Disease," *NIDA Notes* vol. 14, no. 2 (1999).

15. *Epidemiologic Trends in Drug Abuse*. (See note 13 on page 263.)

16. T. T. Gegax and S. Van Boven, "Heroin High," *Newsweek*, 1 February 1999.

17. "Heroin Snorters Risk Transition to Injection Drug Use and Infectious Disease." (See note 14 on page 263.)

18. U.S. Department of Health and Human Services, National Institutes of Health, National Institute on Drug Abuse, *Prescription Drugs: Abuse and Addiction*, Research Report Series (July 2001). NIH publication no. 01–4881.

19. Ibid.

20. A. Hutchinson. Statement of Asa Hutchinson, administrator, Drug Enforcement Administration before the House Committee on Appropriations Subcommittee on Commerce, Justice, State, and Judiciary, 11 December 2001. Available on-line at www.dea.gov/pubs/testimony.htm.

Chapter 11:
Inhalants/Solvents

1. U.S. Department of Health and Human Services, National Institutes of Health, National Institute on Drug Abuse, *NIDA Research Report—Inhalant Abuse* (Rockville, Md.: DHHS, 1994). NIH publication no. 94–3818.

2. National Inhalant Prevention Coalition, *Inhalants—The Silent Epidemic* (Austin, Tex.: Synergies, 1996); M. A. Groves, *Sniffing and Huffing: A Comprehensive Guide for the Prevention and Treatment of Children's Inhalant Abuse* (Minneapolis: The Eden Statewide Children's Chemical Health Services Project, 1996).

3. *Sniffing and Huffing*. (See note 2 above.)

4. Committee on Substance Abuse and Committee on Native American Child Health, "Inhalant Abuse," *Pediatrics* vol. 97, no. 3 (1996).

5. U.S. Department of Health and Human Services, Substance Abuse and Mental Health Services Administration, Office of Applied Studies, *Summary of Findings from the 2000 National Household Survey on Drug Abuse*, NHSDA Series: H–13 (Rockville, Md.: DHHS, 2001). DHHS publication no. (SMA) 01–3549.

6. Ibid.

7. 2001 Monitoring the Future Study, Institute for Social Research, University of Michigan.

8. U.S. Department of Health and Human Services, Substance Abuse and Mental Health Services Administration, Office of Applied Studies, *Emergency Department Trends from the Drug Abuse Warning Network, Preliminary Estimates January–June 2001 with Revised Estimates 1994 to 2000*, DAWN Series: D–20 (Rockville, Md.: DHHS, 2002). DHHS publication no. (SMA) 02–3634.

9. U.S. Department of Health and Human Services, Substance Abuse and Mental Health Services Administration, Office of Applied Studies, *Treatment Episode Data Set (TEDS) 1994–1999, National Admissions to Substance Abuse Treatment Services*, DASIS Series: S–14 (Rockville, Md.: DHHS, 2001). DHHS publication no. (SMA) 01–3550.

10. Ibid.

11. *Inhalants—The Silent Epidemic; Sniffing and Huffing.* (See note 2 on page 264.)

Chapter 12:
Marijuana

1. U.S. Department of Justice, Drug Enforcement Administration, *Drugs of Abuse* (Washington, D.C.: GPO, 1996).

2. Ibid.

3. U.S. Department of Health and Human Services, National Institutes of Health, National Institute on Drug Abuse, *Marijuana: Facts Parents Need to Know* (Rockville, Md.: DHHS, 1995). NIH publication no. 95–4036.

4. U.S. Department of Health and Human Services, National Institutes of Health, National Institute on Drug Abuse, "Marijuana Impairs Driving-Related Skills and Workplace Performance," *NIDA Notes* vol. 11, no. 1 (1996).

5. U.S. Department of Health and Human Services, National Institutes of Health, National Institute on Drug Abuse, *Conference Highlights: National Conference on Marijuana Use: Prevention, Treatment, and Research* (Rockville, Md.: DHHS, 1996). NIH publication no. 96–4106.

6. Ibid.

7. U.S. Department of Health and Human Services, National Institutes of Health, National Institute on Drug Abuse, "Evidence Accumulates That Long-Term Marijuana Users Experience Withdrawal," *NIDA Notes* vol. 15, no. 1 (2000); American Psychiatric Association, *Diagnostic and Statistical Manual of Mental Disorders*, 4th ed. (DSM-IV) (Washington, D.C.: APA, 1994).

8. "Marijuana: Harder Than Thought?" *Science* vol. 276 (27 June 1997); U.S. Department of Health and Human Services, National Institutes of Health, National Institute on Drug Abuse, "Marijuana Antagonist Reveals Evidence of THC Dependence in Rats," *NIDA Notes* vol. 10, no. 6 (1995); U.S. Department of Health and Human Services, National Institutes of Health, National Institute on Drug Abuse, "Researchers Discover Function for Brain's Marijuana-Like Compound," *NIDA News Release* (22 March 1999).

9. *Diagnostic and Statistical Manual of Mental Disorders*. (See note 7 above.)

10. U.S. Department of Health and Human Services, Substance Abuse and Mental Health Services Administration, Office of Applied Studies, *Treatment Episode Data Set (TEDS) 1994–1999, National Admissions to Substance Abuse Treatment Services*, DASIS Series: S–14 (Rockville, Md.: DHHS, 2001). DHHS publication no. (SMA) 01–3550.

11. U.S. Department of Health and Human Services, Substance Abuse and Mental Health Services Administration, Office of

Applied Studies, *Summary of Findings from the 2000 National Household Survey on Drug Abuse*, NHSDA Series: H–13 (Rockville, Md.: DHHS, 2001). DHHS publication no. (SMA) 01–3549.

12. Ibid.

13. 2001 Monitoring the Future Study, Institute for Social Research, University of Michigan.

14. Ibid.

15. U.S. Department of Health and Human Services, Substance Abuse and Mental Health Services Administration, Office of Applied Studies, *Emergency Department Trends from the Drug Abuse Warning Network, Preliminary Estimates January–June 2001 with Revised Estimates 1994 to 2000*, DAWN Series: D–20 (Rockville, Md.: DHHS, 2002). DHHS publication no. (SMA) 02–3634.

16. *Treatment Episode Data Set (TEDS) 1994–1999*. (See note 10 on page 266.)

17. Ibid.

18. Ibid.

19. U.S. Department of Health and Human Services, National Institutes of Health, National Institute on Drug Abuse, *Epidemiologic Trends in Drug Abuse: Volume II—Proceedings of the Community Epidemiology Work Group, June 1998* (Rockville, Md.: DHHS, 1999). NIH publication no. 99–4301.

20. Minnesota Department of Human Services, Performance Measurement and Quality Improvement Division, "Minneapolis Youth Talk About Marijuana," *Research News* (St. Paul: State of Minnesota, 1997).

21. Texas Commission on Alcohol and Drug Abuse, "Fry: A Study of Adolescents' Use of Embalming Fluid with Marijuana and Tobacco," *TCADA Research Brief* (Austin, Tex.: TCADA, 1998).

22. U.S. Department of Justice, Drug Enforcement Administration, *DEA Briefing Book*. Available on-line at www.usdoj.gov/dea/briefingbook (accessed 6 February 2000).

23. Ibid.

24. The National Center on Addiction and Substance Abuse, *Non-Medical Marijuana—Rite of Passage or Russian Roulette?* Press Release (New York: Columbia University, 13 July 1999).

25. J. E. Joy, S. J. Watson, and J. A. Benson, eds., *Marijuana and Medicine: Assessing the Science Base* (Washington, D.C.: National Academy Press, 1999). News release and the executive summary are available on-line at www.nationalacademies.org/news.nsf and www.nap.edu/catalog/6376.html (accessed 29 May 2000).

26. U.S. Department of Health and Human Services, National Institutes of Health, National Institute on Drug Abuse, "Student Use of Marijuana Linked to Perception of Risk," *NIDA Notes* vol. 14, no. 4 (1999); J. Bachman, L. D. Johnston, and P. M. O'Malley, "Explaining Recent Increases in Students' Marijuana Use: Impacts of Perceived Risks and Disapproval, 1976 through 1996," *American Journal of Public Health* vol. 88, no. 6 (1998).

Chapter 13:
Methamphetamine/Stimulants

1. U.S. Department of Justice, Drug Enforcement Administration, *Drugs of Abuse* (Washington D.C.: GPO, 1996).

2. U.S. Department of Justice, Drug Enforcement Administration, congressional testimony of Terrance Woodworth, Deputy Director, Office of Diversion Control, on 16 May 2000, to the Committee on Education and the Workforce, Subcommittee on Early Childhood, Youth, and Families. Available on-line at www.usdoj.gov/dea/pubs.

3. Ibid.

4. U.S. Department of Justice, Drug Enforcement Administration, *Stimulant Use in the Treatment of ADHD*, Conference Report from San Antonio, Texas (10–12 December 1996).

5. D. A. Miller, "Attention Deficit/Hyperactivity Disorder and the Addictive Brain," *Treatment Today* (Fall 1996); and "The Run

on Ritalin: Attention Deficit Disorder and Stimulant Treatment in the 1990s," *Hastings Center Report* vol. 26, no. 2 (1996).

6. U.S. Department of Health and Human Services, National Institutes of Health, National Institute on Drug Abuse, "Methylphenidate (Ritalin)," NIDA InfoFacts no. 13555 (5 November 1999).

7. Congressional testimony of Terrance Woodworth. (See note 2 on page 268.)

8. White House Office of National Drug Control Policy, Drug Policy Information Clearinghouse, *Methamphetamine: Facts and Figures* (Washington, D.C.: GPO, 1997).

9. A. Milosevic, N. Agrawal, P. Redfearn, and L. Mair, "The Occurrence of Toothwear in Users of Ecstasy (3,4 Methylene-DioxyMethAmphetamine)," *Community Dentistry and Oral Epidemiology* vol. 27 (1999): 283–87.

10. U.S Department of Justice, Drug Enforcement Administration, Intelligence Division, "An Overview of Club Drugs," *Drug Intelligence Brief* (February 2000).

11. U.S. Department of Justice, Drug Enforcement Administration, *DEA Briefs and Backgrounds, MDMA and Other Phenelthylamines.* Available on-line at www.usdoj.gov/dea/concern/mdma (accessed 18 July 2002).

12. U.S. Department of Justice, National Drug Intelligence Center, *Effects of D-Methamphetamine: Baseline Assessment, Mexico Unit* (Washington, D.C.: GPO, 1996).

13. U.S. Department of Health and Human Services, National Institutes of Health, National Institute on Drug Abuse, "Methamphetamine Abuse and Addiction," *National Institute on Drug Abuse Research Report Series* (Washington, D.C.: GPO, 1998). NIH publication no. 98–4210.

14. U.S. Department of Health and Human Services, Substance Abuse and Mental Health Services Administration, Center for Substance Abuse Treatment, *Proceedings of the National Consensus*

Meeting on the Use, Abuse and Sequelae of Abuse of Methamphetamine with Implications for Prevention, Treatment and Research (Rockville, Md.: DHHS, 1997). DHHS publication no. (SMA) 97–8013; U.S. Department of Health and Human Services, National Institutes of Health, National Institute on Drug Abuse, "Methamphetamine Abuse Linked to Long-Term Damage to Brain Cells," *NIDA News Release* (27 March 2000).

15. U.S. Department of Health and Human Services, National Institutes of Health, National Institute on Drug Abuse, "Long-Term Brain Injury from Use of Ecstasy," *NIDA News Release* (14 June 1999).

16. U.S. Department of Health and Human Services, Substance Abuse and Mental Health Services Administration, Office of Applied Studies, *Summary of Findings from the 2000 National Household Survey on Drug Abuse*, NHSDA Series: H–13 (Rockville, Md.: DHHS, 2001). DHHS publication no. (SMA) 01–3549.

17. 2001 Monitoring the Future Study, Institute for Social Research, University of Michigan.

18. U.S. Department of Health and Human Services, Substance Abuse and Mental Health Services Administration, Office of Applied Studies, *Emergency Department Trends from the Drug Abuse Warning Network, Preliminary Estimates January–June 2001 with Revised Estimates 1994 to 2000*, DAWN Series: D–20 (Rockville, Md.: DHHS, 2002). DHHS publication no. (SMA) 02–3634.

19. U.S. Department of Health and Human Services, Substance Abuse and Mental Health Services Administration, Office of Applied Studies, *Treatment Episode Data Set (TEDS) 1994–1999, National Admissions to Substance Abuse Treatment Services*, DASIS Series: S–14 (Rockville, Md.: DHHS, 2001). DHHS publication no. (SMA) 01–3550.

20. U.S. Department of Justice, Drug Enforcement Administration, DEA Briefs and Backgrounds, *MDMA and Other Phenelthylamines*. Available on-line at www.usdoj.gov/dea/concern/mdma (accessed 18 July 2002).

Chapter 14:
Sedatives/Hypnotics

1. U.S. Department of Justice, Drug Enforcement Administration, *Drugs of Abuse* (Washington, D.C.: GPO, 1996).

2. Executive Office of the President, White House Office of National Drug Control Policy, *Fact Sheet: Rohypnol* (Washington, D.C.: GPO, June 1998). Publication no. NCJ–161843. Available on-line at www.whitehousedrugpolicy.gov/drugfact/factsheet.html (accessed 22 May 2000).

3. U.S. Department of Justice, Drug Enforcement Administration, Office of Diversion Control, "Flunitrazepam," *Drug and Chemical Evaluation Section* (Washington, D.C.: GPO, 1999).

4. Executive Office of the President, White House Office of National Drug Control Policy, *Fact Sheet: Gamma Hydroxybutyrate (GHB)* (Washington, D.C.: GPO, November 1999). Publication no. NCJ–172867. Available on-line at www.whitehousedrugpolicy.gov/drugfact/factsheet.html (accessed 22 May 2000).

5. U.S. Department of Justice, Drug Enforcement Administration, Office of Diversion Control, "Gamma Hydroxybutyric Acid," *Drug and Chemical Evaluation Section* (Washington, D.C.: GPO, January 2000).

6. U.S. Department of Health and Human Services, Substance Abuse and Mental Health Services Administration, Office of Applied Studies, *Summary of Findings from the 2000 National Household Survey on Drug Abuse*, NHSDA Series: H–13 (Rockville, Md.: DHHS, 2001). DHHS publication no. (SMA) 01–3549.

7. 2001 Monitoring the Future Study, Institute for Social Research, University of Michigan.

8. U.S. Department of Health and Human Services, Substance Abuse and Mental Health Services Administration, Office of Applied Studies, *Emergency Department Trends from the Drug Abuse Warning Network, Preliminary Estimates January–June 2001 with*

Revised Estimates 1994 to 2000, DAWN Series: D–20 (Rockville, Md.: DHHS, 2002). DHHS publication no. (SMA) 02–3634.

9. U.S. Department of Health and Human Services, Substance Abuse and Mental Health Services Administration, Office of Applied Studies, *Treatment Episode Data Set (TEDS) 1994–1999, National Admissions to Substance Abuse Treatment Services*, DASIS Series: S–14 (Rockville, Md.: DHHS, 2001). DHHS publication no. (SMA) 01–3550.

10. U.S. Department of Health and Human Services, U.S. Food and Drug Administration, "FDA Warns About Products Containing Gamma Butyrolactone or GBL and Asks Companies to Issue a Recall," *FDA Talk Paper* T99–5 (Rockville, Md.: DHHS, 21 January 1999); U.S. Department of Health and Human Services, U.S. Food and Drug Administration, "FDA Warns About GBL-Related Products," *FDA Talk Paper* T99–21 (Rockville, Md.: DHHS, 11 May 1999).

11. U.S. Department of Health and Human Services, U.S. Food and Drug Administration, "Important Message for Health Professionals: Report Serious Adverse Events Associated with Dietary Supplements Containing GBL, GHB, or BD," *MedWatch* (25 August 1999).

12. U.S. Department of Justice, Drug Enforcement Administration, 21 CFR, parts 1301 and 1308, "Schedules of Controlled Substances: Addition of GHB to Schedule I," *Federal Register* vol. 65, no. 49 (13 March 2000).

13. U.S. Department of Health and Human Services, National Institutes of Health, National Institute on Drug Abuse, *Epidemiologic Trends in Drug Abuse, Volume II—Proceedings of the Community Epidemiology Work Group, December 1997* (Rockville, Md.: DHHS, 1998). NIH publication no. 98–4298.

14. S. E. Christian, "Teen's Death Sheds Light on Volatile Party Drug," *Chicago Tribune*, 6 February 2000.

15. "Clinton Signs Tough Date Rape Law," *Associated Press*, 18 February 2000.

Chapter 15:
Tobacco

1. National Clearinghouse on Alcohol and Drug Information, "Bidi Fact Sheet." Available on-line at www.health.org/pubs/qdocs/tobacco/bidi2.htm (accessed 14 January 2000).

2. U.S. Department of Health and Human Services, National Institutes of Health, National Institute on Drug Abuse, "Facts About Nicotine and Tobacco Products," *NIDA Notes* vol. 13, no. 3 (1998).

3. U.S Department of Health and Human Services, National Institutes of Health, National Institute on Drug Abuse, "Like Other Drugs of Abuse, Nicotine Disrupts the Brain's Pleasure Circuit," *NIDA Notes* vol. 13, no. 3 (1998).

4. U.S. Department of Health and Human Services, National Institutes of Health, National Institute on Drug Abuse, "Cigarettes and Other Nicotine Products," *NIDA Infofax* no. 13545. Available on-line at www.nida.nih.gov/infofax/tobacco.html (accessed 11 January 2000).

5. U.S. Department of Health and Human Services, National Institutes of Health, National Institute on Drug Abuse, *Nicotine Addiction* (Rockville, Md.: DHHS, 1998). NIH publication no. 98–4342.

6. Ibid.

7. U.S. Department of Health and Human Services, Public Health Service, Centers for Disease Control and Prevention, *Targeting Tobacco Use: The Nation's Leading Cause of Death: At-a-Glance 1999* (Rockville, Md.: Tobacco Information and Prevention Source, 1999). Available on-line at www.cdc.gov/tobacco/oshaag.htm.

8. U.S. Department of Health and Human Services, Public Health Service, Centers for Disease Control, National Center for Chronic Disease Prevention and Health Promotion, Office on Smoking and Health, *The Health Consequences of Smoking—Nicotine*

Addiction: A Report of the Surgeon General (Washington, D.C.: GPO, 1988).

9. U.S. Department of Health and Human Services, Public Health Service, Centers for Disease Control and Prevention, National Center for Chronic Disease Prevention and Health Promotion, Office on Smoking and Health, *Preventing Tobacco Use Among Young People: A Report of the Surgeon General* (Washington, D.C.: GPO, 1994).

10. *Nicotine Addiction.* (See note 5 on page 273.)

11. *Preventing Tobacco Use Among Young People.* (See note 9 above.)

12. *Targeting Tobacco Use.* (See note 7 on page 273.)

13. U.S. Department of Health and Human Services, Substance Abuse and Mental Health Services Administration, Office of Applied Studies, *Summary of Findings from the 2000 National Household Survey on Drug Abuse*, NHSDA Series: H–13 (Rockville, Md.: DHHS, 2001). DHHS publication no. (SMA) 01–3549.

14. Ibid.

15. 2001 Monitoring the Future Study, Institute for Social Research, University of Michigan.

16. U.S. Department of Health and Human Services, Substance Abuse and Mental Health Services Administration, Office of Applied Studies, *Summary of Findings from the 2000 National Household Survey on Drug Abuse*, NHSDA Series: H–13 (Rockville, Md.: DHHS, 2001). DHHS publication no. (SMA) 01–3549.

17. Ibid.

18. U.S. Department of Health and Human Services, Public Health Service, Centers for Disease Control, "Achievements in Public Health, 1900–1999: Tobacco Use—United States, 1900–1999," *Morbidity and Mortality Weekly* vol. 48, no. 43 (1999).

19. R. Kluger, *Ashes to Ashes: America's Hundred-Year Cigarette War, the Public Health, and the Unabashed Triumph of Philip Morris* (New York: Knopf, 1997).

20. S. A. Glantz and A. Charlesworth, "Tourism and Hotel Revenues Before and After Passage of Smoke-Free Restaurant Ordinances," *Journal of the American Medical Association* vol. 281, no. 20 (1999).

Chapter 16:
Other Substances of Abuse

1. T. Chou, "Wake Up and Smell the Coffee: Caffeine, Coffee and the Medical Consequences," *West J Med.* 157 (1992).

2. Ibid.

3. Ibid. G. C. Schreiber, E. E. Maffeo, et al. Measurement of Coffee and Caffeine Intake: Implications for Epidemiologic Research, *Preventive Medicine* vol. 17, no. 3 (1988).

4. U.S. Food and Drug Administration, *An Overview of Dietary Supplements* (January 2001). Available on-line at www.cfsan.fda.gov (accessed 19 July 2002).

5. G. Cowley, "Herbal Warning," *Newsweek*, 6 May 1996.

6. *An Overview of Dietary Supplements.* (See note 4 above.)

7. P. Kurtzweil, "An FDA Guide to Dietary Supplements," *FDA Consumer* (September/October 1998).

8. U.S. Food and Drug Administration, Center for Food Safety and Applied Nutrition, "Consumer Advisory: Kava-Containing Dietary Supplements May Be Associated with Severe Liver Injury," (25 March 2002). Available on-line at www.cfsan.fda.gov~dms/addskava.html (accessed 19 July 2002); U.S. Food and Drug Administration, excerpted from the Special Nutritionals Adverse Event Monitoring System and "Supplements Associated with Injuries," *FDA Consumer* (September/October 1998). Available on-line at vm.cfsan.fda.gov/~dms/qa-sup15.html (accessed 30 May 2000).

9. U.S. Department of Health and Human Services, Food and Drug Administration, "FDA Statement of Street Drugs Containing Botanical Ephedrine," FDA Press Release (10 April 1996).

10. "Survey Finds the Use of Banned Substances Is Up" *The New York Times*, 15 August 2001.

11. U.S. Department of Health and Human Services, National Institutes of Health, National Institute on Drug Abuse, *Drug Abuse Among Athletes*, findings from May 2001 Director's Report. Available on-line at http://165.112.78.61/ICAW/epidemiology/epidemiologyfindings501.html (accessed 17 July 2002).

12. U.S. Department of Health and Human Services, Food and Drug Administration, "FDA Proposes Safety Measures for Ephedrine Dietary Supplements," FDA Press Release (2 June 1997).

13. U.S. Department of Health and Human Services, Food and Drug Administration, Center for Evaluation and Drug Research, Guidance for Industry: Street Drug Alternatives (Rockville, Md.: DHHS, March 2000). Available on-line at www.fda.gov/cder/guidance/index.htm (accessed 12 April 2000).

14. DEWS Alert, "Dextromethorphan (DXM)," *DEA Communicator* vol. 99, no. 1 (Spring 1999).

15. U.S. Department of Justice, Drug Enforcement Administration, Office of Diversion Control, "Dextromethorphan," Drug and Chemical Evaluation Section (Washington, D.C.: GPO, January 1999). DEA/ODE 990115.

16. U.S. Department of Health and Human Services, National Institutes of Health, National Institute on Drug Abuse, *Anabolic Steroid Abuse*, Research Report Series, NIH publication no. 01–3721 (April 2000).

17. Ibid.

18. *Drug Abuse Among Athletes*. (See note 11 above.)

19. U.S. Department of Health and Human Services, National Institutes of Health, National Institute on Drug Abuse, *Anabolic Steroid Abuse*, Research Report Series, NIH publication no. 01–3721 (April 2000).

Index

Index

About the Author

 Carol L. Falkowski, Director of Research Communications at the Hazelden Foundation, has monitored emerging drug abuse trends for nearly twenty years. As one of twenty researchers in the country who participates in an ongoing, national drug abuse surveillance network of the National Institute on Drug Abuse, she regularly analyzes the latest drug-abuse-related data from population surveys, medical examiners, addiction treatment centers, hospital emergency rooms, and law enforcement sources (1986 to present).

Falkowski served in an advisory capacity to the U.S. Food and Drug Administration (1995–1999, 2001) and has provided consultation to numerous states and other national agencies including the National Institute of Justice, the American Bar Association, and the National Drug Intelligence Center. She has published many articles and reports on drug abuse trends and related issues.

As research coordinator at the state alcohol and drug abuse authority in Minnesota, before joining Hazelden in 1997, she designed and implemented a drug abuse monitoring system that served as a model for other states and founded the AIDS/ Substance Abuse Partnership (ASAP). She also directed large-scale, statewide research studies on sentencing, plea negotiation, and court delay in Minnesota's felony courts.

Carol Falkowski was featured in the 1999 Showtime TV documentary by Robert Zemeckis titled *Smoking, Drinking, and Drugging in the Twentieth Century*. She produced a Hazelden video entitled *Addiction, Treatment, and Recovery: A Research Update* and, in 2001, produced and hosted a weekly call-in talk radio show on drug abuse.

As a nationally recognized drug abuse expert, Carol Falkowski has frequent media interviews. She delivers presentations to a variety of professional, academic, and community audiences on topics concerning drug abuse, public policy, and addiction research.

Unrelated to drug abuse, Falkowski wrote and delivered live, on-camera, humorous opening monologues on a weekly public affairs program on the PBS affiliate TV station in Saint Paul, Minnesota, for more than three years.

Carol Falkowski lives in the Minneapolis metropolitan area.